On Creativity, Liberty, Love and the Beauty of the Law

READING AUGUSTINE

Series Editor:
Miles Hollingworth

Reading Augustine offers personal and close readings of St Augustine of Hippo from leading philosophers and religious scholars. Its aim is to make clear Augustine's importance to contemporary thought and to present Augustine not only or primarily as a pre-eminent Christian thinker but as a philosophical, spiritual, literary and intellectual icon of the West.

Volumes in the series:

On Ethics, Politics and Psychology in the Twenty-First Century
John Rist

On Love, Confession, Surrender and the Moral Self
Ian Clausen

On Education, Formation, Citizenship and the Lost Purpose of Learning
Joseph Clair

On Creativity, Liberty, Love and the Beauty of the Law
Todd Breyfogle

On Consumer Culture, Identity, The Church and the Rhetorics of Delight (forthcoming)
Mark Clavier

On Self-Harm, Narcissism, Atonement and the Vulnerable Christ (forthcoming)
David Vincent Meconi

On God, The Soul, Evil and the Rise of Christianity (forthcoming)
John Peter Kenney

On Music, Sound, Affect and Ineffability (forthcoming)
Carol Harrison

On Creativity, Liberty, Love and the Beauty of the Law

Todd Breyfogle

Bloomsbury Academic
An imprint of Bloomsbury Publishing Inc

B L O O M S B U R Y
NEW YORK · LONDON · OXFORD · NEW DELHI · SYDNEY

Bloomsbury Academic
An imprint of Bloomsbury Publishing Inc

1385 Broadway	50 Bedford Square
New York	London
NY 10018	WC1B 3DP
USA	UK

www.bloomsbury.com

BLOOMSBURY and the Diana logo are trademarks of Bloomsbury Publishing Plc

First published 2018

© Todd Breyfogle, 2018

All rights reserved. No part of this publication may be reproduced or transmitted in any form or by any means, electronic or mechanical, including photocopying, recording, or any information storage or retrieval system, without prior permission in writing from the publishers.

No responsibility for loss caused to any individual or organization acting on or refraining from action as a result of the material in this publication can be accepted by Bloomsbury or the author.

Library of Congress Cataloging-in-Publication Data
Names: Breyfogle, Todd, author.
Title: On creativity, liberty, love, and the beauty of the law / Todd Breyfogle.
Description: New York: Bloomsbury Academic, 2017. | Series: Reading Augustine | Includes bibliographical references and index.
Identifiers: LCCN 2017020556 (print) | LCCN 2017039391 (ebook) | ISBN 9781501314056 (ePub) | ISBN 9781501314063 (ePDF) | ISBN 9781501314032 (hardcover : alk. paper)
Subjects: LCSH: Augustine, Saint, Bishop of Hippo.
Classification: LCC BR65.A9 (ebook) | LCC BR65.A9 B74 2017 (print) | DDC 239/.3–dc23
LC record available at https://lccn.loc.gov/2017020556

ISBN:	HB:	978-1-5013-1403-2
	PB:	978-1-5013-1404-9
	ePub:	978-1-5013-1405-6
	ePDF:	978-1-5013-1406-3

Series: Reading Augustine

Cover design: Catherine Wood
Cover image © Dina Alfasi-AyeEm/Getty Images

Typeset by Integra Software Services Pvt. Ltd.

To find out more about our authors and books visit www.bloomsbury.com. Here you will find extracts, author interviews, details of forthcoming events, and the option to sign up for our newsletters.

*In memory of my grandmother,
Myra Briant Humphries, who taught me
more about creativity, liberty, love and beauty
than she—or I—could ever know.
The music of her spirit fills me
like a constant stream.*

*Amor che seppe a te vita serbare
ci sarà guida in terra, e in mar nocchiere,
e vago farà il mondo riguardare,
finché congiunti alle celesti sfere
dileguerem, siccome alte sul mare
al sol cadente, nuvole leggere!*

CONTENTS

Acknowledgements viii
List of Abbreviations x

Prelude 1

1 Echoes of Creation 7
2 The Actor in History 29
3 Righteousness Unbound 43
4 Imagined Communities 61
5 The Arc of Justice and the Arrow of Beauty 83
6 The Music of the Word 101
7 The Law of Liberty and the Law of Love 131

Postlude 145

Bibliography 149
Further Reading 150

ACKNOWLEDGEMENTS

Few things are as beautiful as the gift of time. Like the warmth of sunlight or the first breeze of autumn, the gift of time accompanies us on life's journey—weightless and imperceptible, it leaves its footprints on our souls. This book, both in its content and in its form, bear the footprints of many who have graciously given the gift of their time as a sacred offering. Those offerings have nourished me in countless ways, from the formalities of academic instruction to the gentle gestures of loving friendship. Some did not live to see the conception of this book, but because time does not know the boundaries of life and death they are present in it nonetheless. Many may not be aware of their intellectual and moral contributions, but in thought and example they have helped me understand the beauty of creation's radiant light. Others have provided the space—physical and intellectual—for genuine reflection; still others helped create the spiritual oxygen in which to breathe deeply. All have been and remain my teachers. And all have given me some form of encouragement to understand and write about, however haltingly, and still with much failure, what it means to unfold a lifetime's gift of love.

In this spirit, I express my gratitude to: José M. de Areilza, Olivia Baciu, Ned Barnhart, Dennis Barrett, David Blazquez, Allyson Sudborough Breyfogle, Dave and Pam Breyfogle, Laura Breyfogle, Rob Breyfogle, Miles Brennan, Peter Burnell, Katherine De Chant, Joseph Clair, Jim and Laura Cote, Joseph Cropsey, Robin Darwall-Smith, Amirthanayagam David, Anne David, Wendy Doniger, Helen Durany, Fred and Angelika Fransen, Timothy Fuller, Peter Gilliver, Javier Gomá Lanzón, David Grene, Nicholas Hammond, Marcus Hodges, Stephen and Mary Holley, Miles Hollingworth, Russell Hittinger, Ricardo Iznaola, Zbigniew Janowski, Gareth Jones, Patrick Kelley, Carter Kelton, Fergus Kerr, Beth and George Keys, Cary Kochman, Lezek Kolakowski, Manikandan Kuppan, Jonathan Leathwood, Francesco Leopardi, Jay and Mary Beth

Marshall, Steven McCarl, Neil McLynn, Robert McMahon, Anthony Meredith, Katia Mitova, Mădălina Mocan, Gareth Moore, John and Barbara Morrison, Haaris Naqvi, Carol Neel, James J. O'Donnell, Oliver and Joan O'Donovan, Lavinia Ochea, Kim Orr, Bob Peck, William Craig Rice, Nicholas Hurndall Smith, Hilary Watt Sontag, Jeff and Rebekah Stout, David Tracy, Michael Thaddeus, James Tupper, Richard and Barbara Voorhees, Peter Waanders, Rowan Williams, Robin and Joy Wilson, and David Wroblewski. To these I could add countless students and colleagues, as well as participants in Aspen Institute and other seminars whose conversation and generosity of spirit provide a constant stimulus for thinking about what it means to live justly in a good society.

Finally, I am grateful to my children, Sarah Elisabeth Breyfogle and Lucus Daniel Breyfogle, whose curiosity, kindness, and vitality daily expand the previously unimaginable possibilities of creative liberty. They continue to be my greatest teachers about what it means to love; the beauty of their souls infuses every word I write.

LIST OF ABBREVIATIONS

Works by Augustine

I have used the translations listed, but have regularly referred back to Augustine's Latin, which has a grace and nuance that is often especially difficult to capture in English. Modifications to published translations are identified in the notes and the Latin is easily accessible in the Patrologiae Latinae: *www.augustinus.it/latino/index.htm*

AA	*Against the Academicians*
CG	*City of God*
CF	*Confessions*
LG	*On the Literal Interpretation of Genesis*
MS	*On Music*
FW	*On the Free Choice of the Will*
TC	*On the Teacher*
TR	*On the Trinity*

Other Works

CC	Hannah Arendt, *The Crisis in Culture*
DT	Cicero, *On Duties*
IN	Jean Calvin, *The Institutes of the Christian Religion*
MQ	Ortega y Gasset, *Meditations on Quixote*

Prelude

Love has a song. Only the lover sings. The song stretches forth from the fountain of time, rippling through the currents of the ages like the first rays of sun slipping beneath the sculpted clouds of the eastern horizon. Even the watery clouds have form, coming to be and passing away in the deep blue light, then pink, then full orange, then grey, then white against an infinite blue. Every dawn is a surprise which dawns with predictable regularity. Every morning sings, but sings with a different beauty. We who see the dawn, should we take time to see it, should we wait for and upon it, are likewise different every day—and even more different for resting in the time it takes to wait. The beauty of the dawn does not depend on us, but our perception of its beauty is shaped by the character of our attention, our waiting, our looking at, our beholding. Beauty is not dependent on us, but we are dependent upon the quality of the lens by which we see.

The grace notes of the rays of sun upon the tops of the budding trees of spring, the mist of lakes and valleys, the tops of mountains, set in motion the air currents of the diurnal cycle, rustling leaves, stirring birds, evaporating dew. The quiet songs of night shift to the crescendo of the day, the nocturnal motions yielding to daylight's staccato.

How do we learn to see again? Our lens is clouded—chipped, refracted, distracted, distorted, a fragmentary kaleidoscope of images which dazzle but do not satisfy. How do we learn to hear again? Our hearing is overwhelmed with the chatter of what we want to hear, or the ether which dulls the sound of that which we do not want to hear. These are inhospitable days for preachers and for saints. The preacher cannot row his boat far upstream in today's waters, especially when he has lost his message. And the world is now too cynical for saints, who by definition are imperfect, their saintliness being the refinement of their imperfections even as they overcome them.

Time is not on our side. Rather, we have made enemies of time through our relentless conquest of space. We cannot hear the murmurs of nature or sense the wisdom enfolded in our language, in part because we do not take—we do not make—we do not wait for time; we do not attend to time.

The wisdom of our language grows old with each generation. If this is no age for preachers, it may yet be one for poets. The poet tells us that each generation must articulate the timeless wisdom that has come before, but articulate that wisdom with a new voice. Words crack, sometimes break; they are often shabby equipment, the poet tells us, worn, dried, fragile as fallen leaves in a dry pool. And yet, words are the tools we have for our inarticulate raids into meaning. For it is the beauty of meaning that we seek, not merely information (though we live in an age of information) or knowledge (the age of knowledge, being past, having supplanted the age of wisdom). Where, asks the poet, is the Life we have lost in living? Where is the wisdom we have lost in knowledge? Where he continues, is the knowledge we have lost in information? The times are inauspicious, and we are the perplexed in need of a guide, a guide who can help us see and hear again what the ages have shown and said before, but whose grammar we can no longer recognize as our own. We seek nothing less than a new grammar of the soul.

Who will be our Vergil, a guide through the woods which cannot be navigated easily because of neon light and white noise? Who will walk ahead and alongside us, and behind us as we learn to find our way? We have here not the second great student of Vergil, but the first, himself a kind of Aeneas of the soul in search of a heavenly city.

We walk with Augustine the man and not the saint, for sainthood is not something he himself had chosen. We take Augustine not as our bishop or our preacher, but as a guide in our perplexity. He walks with us not as a furnisher of answers, but as a font of questions. We do not follow him everywhere he leads, though the paths on which we follow him are often overgrown, thin, and difficult to discern. But as those who walk a long trail together talk in words and silence, so with Augustine we follow the conversational trail where it leads, finding perhaps our own way with greater insight and confidence.

This is, then, a journey in conversation, a dialogue—dialogue being one of the few forms of speech adequate to the discernment of meaning. Beyond dialogue, this journey with Augustine is a meditation, a waiting with, a wondering and wandering. Augustine himself recognized—and he is by no means alone—that the processes by which we learn the most important things are not efficient, but stumbling and halting, stops and starts requiring patience, perseverance, and, above all, time. Our meditation, in its failure to travel from one point to another by the shortest possible means, is by no means aimless. That it does not take the form of an academic monograph is deliberate—Augustine is our companion, not our object of the dessications of dispassionate study. This is a meditation with, as well as about, Augustine, but we study him the way we would a friend—not an objectification, but with the objective of greater understanding and love, which, as with any friend, aims not at agreement but at deeper insight.

Genuine learning is a labor of love, and to see the world by entering into another's perspective is to expand our capacity not only for learning but for love. We proceed, then, not in the spirit of academic criticism, but in the spirit of friendship. While informed by scholarship, this meditation with and about Augustine is not an act of scholarship as it has come to be understood. For scholarship demands that we see others and ourselves objectively, as third parties and in the third person, and there can be little intimacy in a relationship defined by distance. Acts of friendship demand of us the vulnerability of friends, the openness, the suspension of disbelief, the eruptions of surprise. Friends have all things in common; friends seek each other's good; and where there is friendship there is no need of justice. Augustine shared this composite Aristotelian wisdom, and in his writings he sought to befriend his readers. In reading him, we seek to return the favor.

It is possible that the recovery of this spirit of writing, or at least of reading, may expand the mind, enlarge the heart, and elevate the soul. Such a mode of writing and reading cannot, then, be an act of academic compliance; and while not exactly an act of rebellion, this meditation with and about Augustine is an experimental act of resistance against the desiccation of the world of thought. Augustine understood that the form of a narrative affects its content. Most of Augustine's non-polemical works defy generic categorization. We undertake our journey with a similar structure and spirit in mind, presenting a thoughtful meditation in an Augustinian voice which is both authentically Augustinian and audible to the contemporary ear. Our journey aims to show rather than tell.

Augustine might, however anachronistically, view our world of thought this way: having left both Athens and Jerusalem behind, the narrowing of reason in the Enlightenment overcorrected the world of faith, substituting logic and the repeatability of natural science in place of an understanding of order and the non-repeatability of the human personality in all its creativity. The reason of the mind triumphed over the reason of mind and heart. Romanticism, in its turn, overcorrected the world of reason, substituting for the objectivity of reason the radical subjectivity of the *sturm und drang* of artistic feeling. The Romantic heart resists, even opposes the order of reason. The postmodern hermeneutics of suspicion views the reason and the heart with mocking restlessness, a cynical, detached ambivalence. Reason and heart, on this view, are seen as nothing other than the simple masks of pernicious power.

These are broad brushstrokes, to be sure, but this brief intellectual history, as it might be seen through an Augustinian lens, crystallizes our predicament as writers and readers in the quest for meaning—can the reason of the mind and the sensibilities of the heart be woven in a harmony which is both loving and not naïve? Can the reasons of the heart break free again in song? Love is a form of knowing. What if the greatest word of all is love?

Law may seem a peculiar compass for our journey. Law for Augustine is a binding command and is therefore inseparable from the question, What binds us together? Augustine links *lex* (law) directly to *ligare* (to bind), the root of the Latin (and our) word "religion." This distinguishes an Augustinian approach to law from the modern, procedural notion that has succeeded Augustine's ancient view. The modern world is preoccupied with civil rights even as we become astonishingly adept at mastering the laws of nature. Reading Augustine, and allowing Augustine to read us, gives us fresh vision in looking at the tension between the regularities of order and the possibilities of creative freedom. Law, for Augustine, is a binding command which manifests itself in the order of nature and the civil order alike. Augustine's account of creation puts human beings—and human freedom—at the center of the cosmic order as the pinnacle of perfection, not in fact but in possibility. To understand Augustine's account of law is to understand human beings as participating in the fashioning of beauty, the reconciliation of matter and spirit, of the disparate parts of existence into a more or less coherent image of fittingness and proportion. It is in this spirit that Augustine can say both "the law of liberty is the law of love" and "love and do what you will."

In reading Augustine and allowing Augustine to read us, we come to see law from a new angle—the aesthetic considerations of what is fitting and proportionate. Beauty helps guide our reading of Augustine and serves as a fresh initiation into an Augustinian way of thinking. Even as we read Augustine, Augustine reads us and forces us to reconsider, to reimagine the contemporary order of things. With any luck, our journey will enact an Augustinian conception of beauty even as it tells about it. What is it that binds us together, individually (as coherent selves), socially (as coherent communities), and spiritually (as beings among many beings in the vast intimacy of space and time)?

Let us walk, now, with steady feet. Augustine will do much of the talking, and sometimes at length, for we are interested in both what he says and how he says it. And as we listen to Augustine, as we learn how to hear again, we also learn how to read him. Sometimes, we will attend to the broad sweep of complete works, like reaching the vista over a valley from a peak or an open ridge. At other times, we will look in detail at small passages, as though finding ourselves in the endless variety of a micro-climate, each specimen forming an essential element in an ecosystem of ideas and expression. Throughout we will attend to the deeper structures of Augustine's thought, the frameworks of his thinking. Indeed, providing frameworks for our own thinking as well as his is part of Augustine's pedagogical method—he presents himself as a weaver of ideas upon the warp and woof of first things. By the end of our journey, we may have found overlapping tapestries, with inconsistent vocabularies, and variable grammars, but in the act of following the weave we have strengthened the fibers of our own souls. Our hearts and minds become richer resonance chambers for the strings that play the song of love.

1

Echoes of Creation

"The beauty of the ages is unfolded by the coming and passing of things" (LG 1.8.4, p. 27). The echoes of the ages are the ripples of change, of the transition from one thing to another, the coming to be of things, and their passing away. Where do we come from? Where are we going? The beauty of the ages haunts us with the mysteries of our origins and our ends.

What binds the flux of creation together in its unfolding? Augustine's verb, "unfolded," is *contexo*: to weave, entwine, braid, to make, construct, join together, form. The ages are indeed beautiful because the things that emerge and fade in time are interwoven, are joined, in and by beauty. Whether the works of creation are material or spiritual, their goodness is aesthetic as well as moral. God is the architect of beauty.

Augustine's *On the Literal Interpretation of Genesis* is a meditation on the architecture of beauty in time. The things of the ages are by definition subject to time, each creature having a proper span allotted to it. And yet, in spite of this temporality—indeed, because of it—God calls all things in creation Good. "God finds pleasure in all the limited perfections of His creatures" (LG 1.6.12, p. 26). We are limited not only in time, but also in form. To have one form is not to have another. One capacity entails an incapacity—those who have wings to fly do not have hooves by which to run. Our beauty consists in the limitation of our perfections. God finds pleasure in our "unfinished state" (LG 1.7.13, p. 26).

The echoes of creation express the priority of form—what it means to have form, to be given form, to turn or be turned from formlessness to form. To speak of "limited perfections" is to acknowledge that in any making, form and substance cannot be separated; they are intertwined. And yet, every creation is a separation, beginning with Genesis' account of the separation of heaven and earth, of the waters and the dry land. "Night certainly consists of darkness that is well ordered" in its separation from light and day (LG 1.17.32, p. 39). To be is not to be something else, and yet to be well ordered.

Augustine cannot separate his meditations on the forms of creation from the form of the narration of creation. The form of creation in Genesis is speech—more precisely, word. Words, like creatures, are at once intertwined and separate—speech makes sense only in the coming to be and passing away of syllables in time. Investigating the creation of things demands an inquiry into the narration of the creation of things and their natures. To be is to be already part of a cosmic story. The Spirit broods over the words of the text no less than it hovers over the face of the waters. Creation itself is inseparable from the words of its narration.

Augustine's mature reflections on Genesis constantly operate on two levels—the content, as it were, of creation, and the form of scripture's narration. In created being and in language, form and content are inseparable. The activity of interpretation is at once a discovery within the text and a creation in the imagination. Any creation of the ages is, however, never a creation ex nihilo, but only a formation, a more well-ordered or coherent rendering of what was previously more formless than formed. Interpretation is both the discovery of intrinsic order and the creative ordering to coherence of that which is initially opaque.

There are at least four levels of the word in Augustine's meditation on creation: the unspoken word before creation, the word spoken at creation, the written word as recorded in scripture, and the interpreted word in exegesis. To these four may be added a fifth: the interpreted word heard and understood (or misunderstood).

Whether in the narration of the word or in creation itself, the things of the ages pivot around form: formless spirit and matter are turned toward (*conversio*) true Being. That which is so turned "receives its proper form and becomes a perfect creature" (LG 1.4.9, p. 23). Augustine calls us to understand the Divine *fiat* as "an immaterial utterance of God in His eternal Word, as the Word recalls His imperfect creature to Himself, so that it may not be formless, but may be formed according to the various works of creation which He produces in due order." In this "conversion and formation (*conversio et formatio*)" the creature imitates the exemplar of the Divine Word (LG 1.4.9, p. 23).

Like an ellipse defined by two foci, form is defined by two divine actions, one of God the Father, the other of God the Son. God the Father creates formless matter ex nihilo, and then gives form to each creature in its limited perfection. To God the Son, as the Word, "belongs the perfecting of created being, which is called back to Him and formed by a union with its Creator and by an imitation, in its own way, of the Divine Exemplar" (LG 1.4.9, p. 24). We are created (by the Father) in a good but unfinished state in anticipation of further formation (by the Son) to our finished state.

The natural movement of the beauty of the ages is from unfinished to finished perfection. The continued perfection of our created nature is itself natural. It is not a product of the fall. Sin is not only the corruption of our created nature; it is a corruption of the natural motion toward the finished perfection for which we were created. We are polished by the Word, not because of the scratches of sin, but so that the imperfect grain of our created natures may shine with greater depth and fullness.

God loves creation "with two purposes": that it may exist, and that it may abide (LG 1.8.14, p. 27). There is a Trinitarian motion in this twofold purpose. God the Father causes things to be. God the Spirit helps things abide. God the Son is that in and by which creatures come to be in the beginning, and that in and by whom creatures come to the fullness of their perfection. Having been given form, it is nonetheless possible to "have a formless life." Living is not the same as "living wisely and happily." For when a creature

> is turned away from changeless Wisdom, its life is full of folly and wretchedness, and so it is in an unformed state. Its formation consists in its turning to the changeless light of Wisdom, the Word of God. The Word is the source of whatever being and life it has, and to the Word it must turn in order to live wisely and happily. (LG 1.5.10, p. 24)

It is not simply enough to be formed. The form must be sustained in order to be perfected. To be perfected in wisdom is to be governed by reason. The *rationes*—rational seeds of order—are "intelligible utterances" of the Word, of Wisdom, "impressed" upon the intellect that allow creatures to be formed and governed (*administratio*) (LG

1.9.17, p. 29). The Father creates according to these *rationes*; the Son forms creatures toward these *rationes*; the Spirit sustains or administers creation by means of these *rationes*.

In the order of time, these *rationes* are experienced as the laws of nature and creation which regulate all material and spiritual movement in the temporal order. Whereas all other material creatures seem not to be able to disobey these laws, human beings as part of their limited perfection have the capacity to deviate from their created form to live a formless life.

God simultaneously created formless matter ex nihilo and gave it form—both in its parts and as a whole. The laws of nature tend toward form in the ongoing birth and growth of creatures, and tend toward formlessness in creatures' dissolution and death over the course of time. That is, the world in the course of time is a complexity of change and non-conformity, just as "mountainous waves are raised up, they are levelled off again with the passing of the storm." Created being may change form, but may not lose form altogether. "Matter is not entirely unformed if it has the appearance of a cloud" (LG 1.12.26-27, p. 34).

Words too are in flux, are not fixed, and yet are never entirely without some intelligible form. To discern our form, to understand our end, we look to our beginnings as recorded in sacred scripture. Augustine's premise is that every utterance is "produced by the speaker for the benefit of the sense of hearing in the ear of the hearer" (LG 1.9.17, p. 28). When God says, "Let there be light!," God does so not only in creative *fiat*, but for our benefit. Even then we are not present to hear the words immediately; we hear the words as mediated through the human authors of scripture. The author of Genesis (Augustine presumes a singular author) "is able to separate in the time of his narrative what God did not separate in time in His creative act" (LG 1.15.29, p. 36). God speaks "with no division of syllables" and yet we can only hear those worlds in discrete syllables, as the sounds come into being and pass away (LG 1.10.19, p. 29). What is unified in eternity is recorded and understood only sequentially in the course of time. Just as timelessness and time are different orders, so too creation and the narrative of creation cannot correspond one-to-one in time; the narrative cannot express the simultaneity of the Divine act.

Augustine assumes the human author of the creation narrative to have the spiritual sensitivity to express himself in accurate words adequate to the unlearned and learned alike. Scripture is intelligible both to those who hear and believe and to those who ponder and explore (LG 1.14.28, p. 35). In what often seems an unnecessarily arcane discussion of scriptural minutiae in *On the Literal Interpretation of Genesis*, it is clear nonetheless that Augustine has a twofold purpose. He is both contending with myriad interpretations circulating at the time—most of which seem highly speculative and untethered from the text—and modeling a way of reading.

Indeed, Augustine says that he wishes to pursue first the literal interpretation as a counterweight to those prevailing spiritual, allegorical, or prophetic interpretations which stray too far (or too soon) from the text. This speculation is, in Augustine's judgment, at best not spiritually nourishing and at worst downright divisive. "Restless and incompetent expounders of Holy Scripture bring untold trouble and sorrow about their wiser brethren," especially when they recite passages from scripture as "proof."

Others, he says, bring the Christian faith into disrepute with non-Christians or those weak in the faith when they maintain, through foolish interpretation, opinions about the workings of the natural world which are clearly not in accordance with "reason and experience." Where there is "reliable evidence" concerning some fact of physical science, the burden is on Christians to show how it is not contrary to scripture. We know things about "the earth, the heavens, and the other elements of this world, about the motion and orbit of the stars and even their size and relative positions," about eclipses, the seasons, "animals, shrubs, stones, and so forth." If Christians "talk nonsense" on these topics, how are they to be taken seriously on matters of much greater significance and ambiguity, such as resurrection and eternal life? (LG 1.19.39, pp. 42, 43; cf. LG 1.21.42, p. 45).

In combatting false or unhelpful opinion, Augustine models a different pedagogy of reading altogether—a patient way of reading scripture that attends to the text. He is teaching us, by his own example, how to read with a disposition to be formed as well as informed. Scripture, for Augustine, manifests a twofold complexity: the difficulty of attending to the narration of the timeless in time, and the apparently deliberately obscure narration designed to nourish our souls "for the purpose of stimulating our thoughts" (LG 1.20.40, p. 43). Scripture too, as the human record in time of divine action outside of time, has its limited perfection; its necessary obscurity is an occasion for greater inquiry and growth. So much of Augustine's treatment of Genesis, and Scripture in general, is the constant questioning of meaning, the testing of various interpretations, the dismissal of some conclusions as unnourishing or inconsistent with "that which our faith demands," and the embrace of multiple interpretations, even if he expresses a preference for one over the other.

The criteria of interpretation emerge. First, choose the interpretation most reasonably intended by the author. Where there is ambiguity, keep to the context of Scripture and the harmony of faith. "For it is one thing to fail to recognize the primary meaning of the writer, and another to depart from the norms of religious belief. If both these difficulties are avoided, the reader gets full profit from his reading" (LG 1.21.42, p. 45). A reader should keep with his powers of understanding and "choose the interpretation that he can grasp" (LG 1.20.40, p. 44). In this advice, Augustine takes vehement exception to those critics who, "full of worldly learning," use that knowledge to quarrel about interpretations of scripture to which they do not adhere but which nonetheless nourish the souls of others. "Such critics are like wingless creatures that crawl upon the earth and, while soaring no higher than the leap of a frog, mock the birds in their nests above."

Second, when interpretations vary, charity and spiritual nourishment should be the criteria, not misapplied erudition, which causes those to turn away who instead should "drink from these books with relish" (LG 1.20.40, p. 44). Scripture read intelligently with a spiritual disposition is like a wheat field. Those who turn away "long for the blossoms on the thorn .... And thus they are idle, though they have permission from the Lord to pluck the ears of grain and to work them in their hands and grind them and winnow them until they arrive at the nourishing kernel" (LG 1.20.40, p. 44).

Both in reading and in writing, Augustine strives for a truth that nourishes, recognizing that even his writing may be subject to multiple interpretations, many of which he cannot have intended or anticipated. To have explored the Genesis narrative, to have dismissed some and considered many interpretations without having settled on a definitive interpretation, is still to have nourished the soul. We are to brood over the text the way the Spirit has brooded over the face of the waters, just like "a bird that broods over its eggs, the mother somehow helping in the development of her young by the warmth from her body, through an affection similar to that of love" (LG 1.18.36, p. 41).

In brooding over the text with the warmth of charity, Augustine is keen to tease out the order in which things are created as well as the relation of their qualities. Indeed, the beauty of the ages is unfolded not only in the mosaic of time but also in the quilt of quality—the individual characteristics of each created being and the complementarity of each to the other as part of a composite whole. At this stage of Augustine's account, he addresses the qualities of species, or of substances, not of physical individuals. But, as we shall see, the complementarity of species comes to apply also to the complementarity of individuals in manifesting unique unfolding potential. But we get ahead of ourselves.

The unfolding of the cosmos in time is interwoven with the unfolding of the word in the narration of creation. Augustine's engagement with the two books of creation and scripture is an extended meditation on form: how do we discern the intelligibility of an order—physical, spiritual, verbal—of things coming to be and passing away?

In the grammar of creation there are three unfoldings simultaneously—the unfolding of nature, the unfolding of the text, and the unfolding of the meditative reading on the part of the learner. The text is at once the object being viewed (the mediated account of creation) and the lens by which creation is being viewed. The text is both a reflection of creation and an occasion for reflection on creation. As we unfold the meaning of the text, we refine our perception of the unfolding of the created order, and in turn our souls are unfolded through a meditative reading that borders on prayer.

What nourishing kernels might be plucked from the account of the six days of creation? While he treats the six days chronologically (as we would put it), Augustine is careful to emphasize that the narration of creation is really logical, not chronological. God created all things simultaneously, and yet, just as we cannot pronounce a multisyllabic word in one instant, so too the narrative of creation must proceed one step at a time. We are invited to view the account of the six days of creation as a logical description, not as a chronological one (LG 4.32.49-4.35.56, pp. 139–45).

Creation has several logical steps: the creation of formless matter ex nihilo, the formation of formless matter into forms (species), and the formation of species into individuals. Here the tension between the logical and the chronological becomes clearer. What would it mean to have formless matter? And if we could imagine such a thing, we cannot hold (Augustine maintains) that God created by giving form to matter which pre-existed alongside the divine. (In Plato's *Timaeus*, the Demiurge forms the world out of pre-existing matter.) Similarly, what would it mean to have a species without an individual? Or vice versa? No, creation and formation must be a simultaneous act, Augustine insists.

And yet, the human author of the Genesis narrative gives us an account of creation over six days. In a repetitive narrative form, each day creation is described according to the rhythm of the day, the evening, and the morning. And each day God says that the creation is good. How can this account nourish our souls?

In his attention to intrinsic order, Augustine observes that the six days of creation reflect the perfection of the number six, which is uniquely both the sum and the product of its parts (LG 4.2.2-5, pp. 104–107). One, two, and three are the foundational primary numbers, and when added or multiplied yield six. And so, Augustine looks for combinations of one, two, and three, and he plays with symmetries, both one to six and one to seven, recognizing that the account of creation cannot be separated from God's rest on the seventh day.

As with his engagement with alternative interpretations, Augustine is curious about questions rather than conclusions, at least in his initial encounters with the text. The fourth day is not central if one is considering the six days of creation, but it is central when considering all seven days of the Genesis narrative. If that is the case, then in what ways does the creation of light on the first day correspond to God's rest on the seventh? And what relation is the creation of the firmament and waters on the second day with that of man on the sixth? (LG 2.13.26-27, pp. 63–65).

Well beyond numeric virtuosity, Augustine is interested in what is unique about each moment of creation and how each part is related to the others. His explorations are a meditative pause, an exegetical contemplation which allows the beauty of creation's structure—and the structure of its narration—to emerge. With other animals, we see the corporeal things of creation, but unlike other animals, incorporeal images present themselves "before the gaze of our souls" as we contemplate mathematical patterns.

Reason "contemplates within itself the nature" of the number six in its divisibility and permanence. Beauty is perceived in a separate, unique way when reason opens itself to aesthetic, non-utilitarian coherence or pattern. The proper response, as Augustine demonstrates, is worship: "Let the spirit of man, then, always give thanks to the Creator, who has created man with the power of seeing what neither bird nor beast can see, although they share with us the sight of sky and earth" (LG 4.7.7, p. 112).

Just as the six days of creation reveal a logic of order and causal relation, so too the rhythm of creation each day suggests its own order. Day, evening, and morning of each day are the beats of the music of creation in the knowledge of the angels. By day, they see the form of the creature in the spirit of the Word; by evening, they see the individual creature in creation, but necessarily with inferior knowledge (as signified by "evening"); by morning, the angels praise God for the knowledge given them in the Word of other creatures to be created (LG 4.31.48, p. 138). Spirit, matter, worship. Angelic knowledge proceeds from the spiritual form to the material body, concluding with worship, for knowledge is incomplete without praise. Human knowledge proceeds in the reverse, beginning with the perception of bodies and proceeding to the understanding of the spiritual form.

The discursive activity of the human mind has four moments, according to Augustine: perception of the physical body, an inquiry into its causes, an understanding of its form, and finally the praise and worship of the Creator. Praise is, as it were, the capstone of the order of knowing. The angelic mind, united as it is to the Word "in pure charity," refers its knowledge of creatures to God. In contrast, the human mind, by virtue of its natural, imperfect unity with the Word, possesses knowledge in two ways: the creature is known in itself and delighted in without reference to God, or the creature is known in itself and delighted in with reference to God (LG 4.32.49, pp. 139, 140).

The scriptural account of creation thus operates in three dimensions, even as it "proceeds slowly step by step" so that human readers may be nourished fully (LG 4.33.52, p. 142). In the logical dimension, all created reality is in unity with the Creator and God's works occur in an instant of simultaneity. In the chronological dimension, there is a narrative sequence in which our discursive minds understand the distinctions of time and space sequentially, rather than simultaneously. In the etiological dimension, we have the discursive understanding of casual sequences (LG 4.34.53-55, pp. 143–45). The logical yields knowledge; the chronological, understanding; the etiological, praise.

Just as Augustine hopes to see for himself, and to help his readers see, the integration of the parts of creation with the whole, so too he is trying to refine our capacities for understanding, to view creation in its logical, chronological, and etiological dimensions simultaneously. In this simultaneity, there is no longer a "before" or "after." As we gaze across the expanse of the ocean, says Augustine, we understand our sight to proceed both sequentially (air, water, light) and simultaneously—we take it all in in an instant. Or when we close our eyes and look at the sun and then open our eyes, we know that the rays of light have traversed "measureless spaces" with "such speed that it cannot be calculated or equaled." And yet, "there will seem to be no lapse of time between the moment we open our eyes and the moment our gaze meets its object" (LG 4.34.54, p. 144).[1]

Augustine is pointing us toward something beyond the mere knowledge of creation and its internal patterns. He is helping us build the muscle of seeing "before" and "after" alongside the moment of eternal singularity. The weakness of our gaze is a function not of sin, but of our limited perfection. To know in ignorance is to be in error, and this is to dwell in darkness. To know in creation (*natura*) is to dwell in the light of evening. To know in God (*ratio*) is to dwell in the light of day (LG 4.23.40, p. 131).

The journey from darkness to evening to light is a turning from the unformed to the formed—formation is a turning to the divine light. Take for example the evening of the first day, in which even the light dwells in its proper form: "Consequently, after evening, morning is made, when after its knowledge of its own nature as something distinct from God, this light directs itself to praise the Light that is God, in the contemplation of which it is formed." As creatures "direct to the praise of their Creator the gift of their

---

[1] Augustine seems to understand light as a particle, but consistent with ancient theories of sight, understood the eye to be the origin of the ray of light, rather than its receptacle.

creation" they receive from the Word of God further knowledge of creation (LG 4.22.39-4.23-40, pp. 129–31). That is, the completion of knowledge in praise ushers in a new morning of encounter with the next phase of creation.

God's creation stops on the sixth day, but the rhythm of knowledge of the day, the evening, and the morning persists in our own encounter with creation. This knowledge is the sequential and simultaneous knowledge of self, of other creatures, and of God, even as we come to see self and others in God. In the absence of praise, we remain in the knowledge of the evening. With praise, the new morning is ushered in and with it, the promise of the freshness of new creation.

Seeing oneself and others in God is to recognize the proper place of each in the order of creation. The touchstone for Augustine is that God "has ordered all things in measure, and number, and weight" (LG 2.1.2, p. 47; the phrase is from Wisd. 11.21). At the most basic level, this means that each created thing has its own unique intrinsic qualities, which in turn determine its physical placement and tendencies. Oil poured into water will rise to the surface. A piece of earth sinks to the bottom. A jar placed upside down in water will not fill up with water. Augustine's physics seems very much like Aristotle's: things tend toward their proper places. God, Augustine says, could will things to be otherwise, but this would be to violate their measure, number, and weight. Creation, therefore, is an expression of reason, not of will.

Indeed, there is a rational limitation to a creature's nature, for "every created nature is confined within its fixed boundaries of origin and limit." Augustine uses the diurnal rhythms of creation as metaphors for the temporal limitations of creatures. "Evening, then, in this sense would be a kind of limit of each creature's perfection, and morning would be the original state from which it would start." Our coming to be and passing away reflect the "orderly cycle of nature" as part of "the beauty of the temporal order" (LG 4.1.1, p. 104).

Measure, number, and order do not exist outside of God; God does not refer to something external when creating.

> But in the sense that measure places a limit on everything, number gives everything form, and weight draws each thing to a state of repose and stability, God is identified with these three

in a fundamental, true, and unique sense. He limits everything, forms everything, and orders everything. Hence, in so far as this matter can be grasped by the heart of man and expressed by his tongue, we must understand that the words, Thou hast ordered all things in measure and number and weight, mean nothing else than "Thou has ordered all things in Thyself." (LG 4.3.7, p. 108)

These things are hard to grasp by the heart, and difficult to express with the tongue. How does one refine the gaze so as to discern the measure, number, and weight of all things? By what words does one give voice to the beauty and the wonder of the apprehension of creation? What does it mean to see all things ordered in God? How does one find the measure beyond measure, the number beyond number, the weight beyond weight? "It is a marvelous gift, granted to few persons, to go beyond all that can be measured and see the Measure without measure, to go beyond all that can be numbered and see the Number without number, and to go beyond all that can be weighed and see the Weight without weight" (LG 4.3.8, p. 108). Creatures are revealed in their measure, number, and weight, and in turn reveal the measureless, numberless, weightless Creator from whom we come.

Measure, number, and weight correspond with limit, form, and repose. These are the features of intrinsic order in space, in time, in spirit. In the realm of matter, oil rises to the surface of water. In the realm of time, created things come into being and decay. In "the realm of spirit or mind," too, creatures are subject to measure, number, and weight—these are not to be thought of as material and temporal only.

> There is also the measure of an activity, which keeps it from going on without control or beyond bounds; there is the number of the affections of the soul and of the virtues, by which the soul is held away from the unformed state of folly and turned towards the form and beauty of wisdom; and there is the weight of the will and of love, wherein appears the worth of everything to be sought, or to be avoided, to be esteemed of greater or lesser value. (LG 4.4.8, p. 109)

From morning to evening in time our activities are governed by limit, form, and repose. What are the principles which limit our activity? What are the affections which form our soul? What are the loves that pull us toward repose? How do we discern what is to be esteemed of greatest value? The journey from morning to evening is an unrehearsed adventure in limit, form, and repose, an experiment in learning how to allow ourselves to be drawn upward—to the measure, number, and weight by which we were created—amid the pull of the beauty of the created order around us.

> Every creature has a special beauty proper to its nature, and when a man ponders the matter well, these creatures are a cause of intense admiration and enthusiastic praise of their all-powerful Maker .... He creates them tiny in body, keen in sense, and full of life, so that we may feel a deeper wonder at the agility of the mosquito on the wing than at the size of a beast of burden on the hoof, and may admire more intensely the works of the smallest ants than the burdens of the camels. (LG 3.10.23, p. 90)

Our love is drawn to praise rather than to possession when we pause to refer the goodness of creatures to their Maker.

This journey from morning to evening begins with an understanding of our proper nature. God has made "the nature proper to each thing." Within that nature, with its limited perfection, reside potential perfections to be unfolded. These unfolding perfections are not new: "whenever a creature in its natural development in due course discloses and puts forth some perfection, this added something was previously hidden within that creature" (LG 2.15.30, p. 68). This would seem to be true not only of human beings, but of other animals, appropriate to their measure, number, and weight. The fish in the large fountain at Bulla Regia, Augustine observes, clearly possess the capacity for memory, as do birds, as manifest "in their chatter as well as in the skill they have in building their nests and training their young" (LG 3.8.12, p. 82). Much more so in human beings, the interplay between reason (limit), intellect (form), and will (love) unfold—to a greater or lesser degree, depending on our choices—the latent perfections within each of our individual natures.

Augustine encourages us to think of the unfolding of latent perfections as the same as the process of formation, of turning toward that which we are called to be. In our acquisition of wisdom, "we go forth to see and understand the invisible things of God through the things that are made" (LG 2.8.17, p. 57). The form of each nature exists in the Word before time; the form of each nature is reformed by the Word in time; the form is perfected by the Word in the time to come. Both our initial and our progressive illumination and formation consist of coming to see more clearly the invisible things of God as manifest in the visible and invisible things of creation, including ourselves.

This movement consists also in moving from the sight of visible things to the contemplation of invisible things. The visible things are evident in the order of time, though "matter unformed and formable, both spiritual and corporeal" came first in creation in the order of causality (LG 5.5.13, p. 154). God knew the measure, number, and weight of all things before creating them. Time itself begins with creation, in the motion of creatures from one state to another in the light of "day."

In the order of causation, all creatures were created on a single day. In the narrative of time, God fashioned the individual beings on the appropriate day of creation. In creating the fish of the sea or the quadrupeds of the land, Augustine maintains, God created individual animals. God also created within those animals the causal principles or rational seeds by which those individuals would propagate, each according to their proper measure, number, and weight. Creation begins with the creation of the form itself in the order of causation and the reception of the form by the individual in time, and continues in the propagation of the form by the unfolding of the causal principles in time (LG 5.5.12-5.23.44, pp. 153–76).

There are, then, "two moments of creation": one in the original creation when God made all creatures before resting on the seventh day, and the other in the administration (*administratio*) "within the course of time" (LG 5.11.27, p. 162). These two moments of creation may be understood under three aspects: the unchangeable forms in the word of God, God's works from which he rested on the seventh day, and the things that God produces from those works according to their intrinsic capacities.

Within the individuals created by God's initial work are the principles of the species and their propagation in time. That is, in creating the individual in the first instance, God creates also the principles (*rationes*) of the species by which each will bring forth more according to their kind. These *rationes*—conceptually very

Order	Material realm	Immaterial realm	God
measure	limit	activity	beyond measure
number	form	virtues of soul	beyond number
weight	repose	love and wisdom	beyond weight

much akin to our current understanding of DNA—continue to unfold in the course of time. Only the third aspect is known to us in some way; the first two "are beyond our senses and ordinary human knowledge" (LG 5.12.28, p. 163). The first two aspects are invisible to us, while in our limited capacity only the third aspect is visible.

"Let us, then, consider the beauty of any tree in its trunk, branches, leaves, and fruit." The tree did not spring forth suddenly in its current size and form, but went through a process of growth and development that we regularly observe. In the seed of the tree, "there was invisibly present all that would develop in time into a tree." But there is no seed without a tree, just as there is no egg without a chicken. The two moments of creation provide Augustine with an elegant solution. God creates the tree, within which exist the *rationes* which, embedded in the seed, allow subsequent trees to unfold in the course of time (LG 5.23.44-45, pp. 174, 175). Time is the working out of the natural possibilities latent in the causal reasons of each creature's measure, number, and weight.

We are ignorant of other natures and of the mind of God. Most creatures "are inaccessible to our mind because, being corporeal, they are of a different nature, and our mind is unable to see them in God, in the archetypes according to which they were made." If we could see them in God, then we would know their measure, number, and weight. In this, God is nearer to us than many of the other things God has made. That God is nearer (more apprehensible) than the nature of creatures qualifies our ignorance, for we are nearer to God by virtue of having been made in God's image (LG 5.16.34, p. 167).

God moves "His whole creation by a hidden power," not by acting on it from without, but by having implanted from the beginning the principles of its unfolding. Augustine rejects both deism and punctuated interventionism—with Darwin, Augustine holds that God does not actively tweak creation. God's continued action is through the order of causation; even as new variations of creatures unfold in time, we must still ascribe their creation to God who made the principles of their unfolding.

> God moves His whole creation by a hidden power, and all creatures are subject to this movement: the angels carry out His commands, the stars move in their courses, the winds blow now this way, now that, deep pools seethe with tumbling waterfalls and mists forming above them, meadows come to life as their seeds put forth grass, animals are born and live their lives according to their proper instincts, the evil are permitted to try the just. It is thus that God unfolds the generations which He laid up in creation when first He founded it; and they would not be sent forth to run their course if He who made creatures ceased to exercise His provident rule over them. (LG 5.20.41, pp. 171, 172)

Augustine insists that God's providence extends to the lowest of the low, and that all of creation has something to teach us. "Creatures shaped and born in time should teach us how we ought to regard them." We are taught not only by the animate of creation but by the inanimate also. We learn from creatures how to regard them by being lovers of the Wisdom by which God made them and according to which God sustains them (LG 5.21.42, p. 172). To grow in regard for creatures is to love them in God, and to grow in our apprehension of "every rule of measures, every harmony of numbers, every order of weights" which come from God (LG 5.22.43, p. 173).

In our ignorance, and in the differentiation of created natures, we tend to regard other creatures as though they are subject to our nature (both our nature as humans and as individuals), rather than to discern and affirm them in their own proper natures. In an anticipation of material scientism, Augustine criticizes those "who think that nothing exists unless they can see it" or that if it does exist, it is "identical in nature with what they have been accustomed to see" (LG 5.22.43, p. 174). We come to understand the unity and beauty of our own natures by lovingly regarding the unity and beauty of the natures of those creatures around us. The natural ecology is also a moral ecology.

Scripture's repetition of the phrase "according to their kinds" refers to "the power of the seed to reproduce a likeness in the offspring of a creature that must perish," for nothing has been made that must not perish. It is in this way that creatures fulfill the command to be fruitful and multiply. But, Augustine observes, the phrase "according to his kind" was not used of human beings, because "only one was created and from him woman was made. For there are not many kinds of men, as there are of crops, trees, fish, birds, reptiles, hers, and wild beasts" which may be classified as species. That is to say, for beasts there are many breeds within one species. For humans, there is only one breed and one species. Human nature possesses a unity and beauty that is unique in creation, a unity which defies divisive classification based on physical variation (LG 3.13.19-20, p. 88).

In the symmetry of creation, human beings are the pinnacle, the keystone of matter and spirit. To say that human beings are the pinnacle is not to make a statement of superiority, but of complexity. Indeed, angelic natures are superior in their spiritual knowledge, just as earthy creatures are superior in their physical abilities. In some sense, superiority is a misleading, indeed deficient, category altogether. For each created nature has its distinct measure, number, and weight. And while there is, for Augustine, a hierarchy in the order of creation, the hierarchy is one of relation, not of dominance by virtue of intrinsic nature. Each created nature tends toward its proper perfection only in relation to the other natures in creation.

Human beings are the keystone, then, in the harmony they bring to the union of matter and spirit, the chords of memory, intellect, and will that are manifest in the love of the Creator *in se*, and in the Creator's self-expression in the wonder of creation. Just as each species has its proper measure, number, and weight, so too each individual—as a unique unfolding of the potential of the species nature in time and space—has his or her own measure, number, and weight. That is, a lion possesses the general qualities of "lion-ness" appropriate to the species *Panthera leo*, and the measure, number, and weight of a specific individual lion in time and space; that is, this lion whom we call "Leo" unfolds generic "lion-ness" subject to his individual experiences and to his unique learned responses to those experiences.

Whether as lions or as human beings, our individual journey is an adventure in learning, an experiment in coming to know our individual measure, number, and weight as we encounter the measure, number, and weight of others, and of others outside of our own species. A dog or a horse has more excellent potentialities unfolded as a consequence of its relationships with human beings, and vice versa. As the keystone of creation, possessing both reason and matter—caught as it were at the junction of the material and the spiritual—our beauty is the most complex of all creatures, earthly and angelic alike. Measure, number, and weight have an intrinsic dimension—my relationship to myself—as well as an extrinsic dimension—my relation to the rest of creation, both in regard to my species and my individual nature. Both intrinsically and extrinsically, I enact my origins and ends, both as the member of a species (the order of causation) and as an individual (the order of time) (LG 4.1.1-4.5.12, pp. 103–11). The specific complexity of the human species is its participation in both a natural and a moral ecology—I can enact my origins and ends, both with respect to myself and to other creatures, well or poorly.

This is the beauty of our created natures, both in the order of causation and in the order of time. We are created to learn, and our learning happens only in the company of others, in concentric circles that ripple out in the encounter with the inanimate, animate, and angelic natures created by God at the dawn of time, as we can discern them in the course of time (history), and in our relationship with the current state of their unfoldment (the present). After each day of creation God saw that the creatures were good, both as parts of creation and with respect to the sum of the parts in a whole. More than good, they are beautiful, and "if individual parts are beautiful, all together making up the organic whole are much more beautiful." To be "very" good, as scripture says, is to be beautiful in parts and wholes.

The introduction of sin is a rupture in the fabric of beauty. But even this rupture cannot take away from creation's ontological beauty. "But creatures that lose their own proper beauty by sinning can in no way undo the fact that even they, considered as part of a world ruled by God's providence, are good when taken with the whole of creation" (LG 3.24.37, p. 102). In sin we lose our proper beauty by misjudging our measure, number, and weight, and in so doing, distort our perception of the measure, number, and weight of others. At the same time, we retain our essential created goodness insofar as we continue to participate in Being.

Without sin, we are engaged in learning our origins and ends as we journey from our limited perfection to the unfoldment of our latent potential. As creature, I am good *in se*, and I am good in my potential to grow in more perfect beauty through the formation for which I was created. With sin, my journey toward more perfect beauty is compromised. Not only is my knowledge not angelic, but my capacity to gaze rightly upon myself and others has been distorted, as it were, by a gravitational field generated by the imbalance of the importance that I place on my own measure, number, and weight. The imbalance can be mitigated by Christ's redemption, but the journey of formation toward a more beautiful perfection is now experienced as a struggle, whereas before it was exclusively a delight. Just as our agricultural labors after the Fall involve toil, so our learning and spiritual cultivation in conditions of sin require sometimes unpleasant exertion. Yet, even in conditions of sin we calibrate our measure, number, and weight in relation to the rest of the created order, which remains, as in God's initial estimation, good. "Hence, whenever creatures individually lose their loveliness by sin," Augustine maintains, "nevertheless the whole of creation with them included always remains beautiful" (LG 3.24.37, p. 102).

As the conjunction of material body and spiritual intelligence, human beings are uniquely self-consciously reflective in their understanding and enactment of their origins and ends. To be human is to have the natural capacity to knowingly and willingly put oneself at odds with the order of creation, to refer the measure, number, and weight of others (including God) to oneself, rather than measuring oneself in reference to the beauty of the whole. Having stumbled into sin, we find our naturally limited capacities for knowing, willing, and loving compromised; this is the equipment by which we learn to find our intrinsic and extrinsic measure, number, and weight. Our experience of internal and external disorder or discord is best described as a restlessness, an ignorance of and resistance to our origins and our ends, a prescinding from the rest for which we were created. Under conditions of sin, the human journey is now a series of halting attempts to recover our original beauty, a now restless adventure to fall into alignment with the divine repose (LG 4.13.24-4.27.44, pp. 119–35).

For rest is perfect form. The passage of time, the coming to be and passing away of things, is a reminder of the rest for which we were created. The works of the six days point toward the Sabbath rest of the seventh. This rest is "the gift of the Holy Spirit" to the rational beings God created. "For as we are justified in saying that God does whatever we do by His operation within us, so we can rightly say that God rests when by His gift we rest" (LG 4.9.16, p. 114). Rest is God's gift in which we come to see the many gifts of creation and, in so doing, become more complete. God rests in the sense that God does not create any new creatures, even while God does not cease sustaining and governing creation by means of the causal principles set in motion by the original works of creation. God's rest, then, is a continued presence in the unfolding of creation (LG 4.12.22-23, p. 117). God's Wisdom "governs created things graciously," giving them a stable motion which is beyond our capacity to comprehend or describe. This ruling (*regendi*) sustains natural motions according to the laws of proper natures, the regulation reflective of our measure, number, and weight (LG 4.12.23, p. 118). Our longing for rest is a desire for peace as *prima natura*, a divine repose of overflowing goodness that our human intellect cannot penetrate (LG 4.14.25-27, pp. 120–22).

Our restlessness in conditions of sin prompts us to find our likeness to God in resting in ourselves and our work. This is a misplaced imitation—being like God in pride, rather than humbly referring our beauty to the source of Beauty. We must rest not in ourselves, but "in an immutable Good, that is, in Him who made us. This will be our most exalted state of rest, a truly holy state, free from all pride." Our likeness to God is to rest in God, and in so doing we become more perfect in our beauty (LG 4.17.29, pp. 122, 123).

In interpreting the days of creation, Augustine takes evening to mean the limit of created nature. The evening of the sixth day is followed by morning of the seventh, to "begin the repose of all creation resting in its Creator." For us, this repose has a beginning but no end in creation, "for the seventh day begins with morning, but no evening ends it." Rest has no limit. Rest is perfect form. Rest is the perfect attention of creature to the creator, a perfection of both our nature and our orientation. "For the perfection of each thing according to the limits of its nature is established in a state of rest, that is, it has a fixed orientation by reason of its natural tendencies, not just in the universe of which it is a part, but more especially in Him to whom it owes its being, in whom the universe itself exists." Our journey from limited perfection has two valances: our created nature—understood in terms of our measure, number, and weight, expressed both in species and individual characteristics—and our orientation—toward self or toward God. We maintain our "nature and identity" only in God; only in God do we find a "place of rest" (LG 4.18.31-35, pp. 123–26).

Even before the Fall, we are created to learn, and so the ecology of creation is seen to be regulated by the injunction to learn to love more fully. Created nature and nature's laws provide the structure for fulfilling our potential as human beings. Ours is a journey of formation to a higher perfection, complicated but not initiated by sin. To be ruled by form is to bend our repining restless toward a more perfect angle of repose.

2

The Actor in History

Creation is the working out of divine rest in time. Time is the arc of our created nature learning to rest more perfectly in God. Human history is the continued, frustrated attempt of our fallen natures to resume the rest for which they were created. Just as nature has an order to be discerned with evening knowledge, so too experience—to be coherent—requires an ordered narrative, an ex post facto assembly of events into patterns of intelligibility which make sense of the past and provide a provisional guide to the future. The Genesis narrative attempts to verbalize the creation of the natural world; history attempts to narrate the unfolding of human nature in time. Because we, with evening knowledge, do not see all things simultaneously, our encounter with living is sequential—we encounter things, others, and ourselves as coming to be and passing away one after another. This is the use of memory, this is the use of imagination: the discernment and invention of patterns of experience in time, just as attention to nature allows patterns of order to disclose themselves and, in so doing, to unveil God.

As with scripture, every narrative begs interpretation. Not only do we interpret nature, we interpret ourselves in our experience—individually, collectively, and in the species. Just as *On the Literal Interpretation of Genesis* explores the structure and unfolding of creation, *The City of God* charts the structure and unfolding of our education in history. Indeed, Augustine maintains, it is beginning with the law given to the children of Israel "that part of the human race that consists of the people of God" has received a "right education." As with a single human being, so too a people can advance in learning, epoch by epoch or age by age, and so "rise upwards from temporal to eternal things, and from the visible to the invisible" (CG 10.14, p. 412).

Nature itself discloses the order of measure, number, and weight. The Law clarifies the sight of our evening knowledge by articulating the scale of value to rest alongside the scale of nature. The gradations of nature proceed from inanimate, to animate, to intelligent, to the immortal. "But here are also various standards of value arising out of the use to which we put this thing or that" (CG 11.16, p. 470). The narratives we invent reflect the standards of value formed by our use of the things of nature. These standards of value in turn form our use of the things of nature. As actors in history, we wrestle to align the values and forms of our narratives with the order of creation.

The contrasts within nature, the contrasts within history, and the contrasts between nature and history are shot through with beauty in the architecture of the divine unfolding in time. History is a narrative in which God the sustainer puts all things to good use, "adorning the course of the ages like a most beautiful poem set off with antitheses .... Just as the opposition of contraries bestows beauty upon language, then, so is the beauty of this world enhanced by the opposition of contraries, composed, as it were, by an eloquence not of words, but of things" (CG 11.18, p. 472).

What does it mean to regard history as a poem, a poem at once epic and lyric, a poem in which we (individually and as a species) compose and participate, telling and retelling, revising with halting rhythms, caesuras, elisions, and alliterations? Our challenge in narrative is to learn, day by day, age by age, to give the disparate elements of experience and nature their proper measure, number, and weight, both in themselves and in relation to one another according to a more refined, more divine, standard of value.

In falling from our original beauty, we humans are able to put ourselves at odds with the order of nature. In our interior dimension, we suffer from the misalignment of knowing, willing, and loving. In our exterior dimension, we find ourselves in misalignment with others and with the natural world. We are, then, engaged in the activity of learning how to order our souls (internally) and order our actions (externally) toward created nature—our social relationships and our actions toward all elements of created nature.

To be the composers and interpreters of the poetry of history is to take up the challenge of understanding the unfolding of our measure, number, and weight in time. This understanding takes place in the twilight between evening and night—our knowledge is compromised, our attention distracted, and our discernment of the patterns of nature is obscured. These are the conditions under which we labor not only to understand the poem of history, but to bring it into some reconciliation with the poem of nature.

Our adventure in poetry has three movements, as it were, three distinct modes or three dramatic loci—what we might call the lyric, the fabulous, and the epic. The lyric is the poetry of the internal ordering of the soul. The fabulous is the poetry of the social, the city. The epic is the poetry of the historical—the journey of the soul and of the city in the course of time. These fields of drama intersect— how we order our souls depends upon the terms of the social and the historical; the drama of city and history in turn are shaped by how we order our souls. We are at once, then, the composers (perhaps, also, compositors) and interpreters of the poetry of the individual, the social, and the species; the drama of each takes place against the backdrop of the grammar of creation.

What are the terms of the interior poem? There are three moments of action, four dispositions of the will, and two qualities of love. The moments of action. The elements recorded in memory become the components of understanding—the intellect arranges the data of memory into a more or less coherent pattern of meaning on which the soul bases an act of will. So, remembering, understanding, and willing form the conjoint motion of the soul, at once sequential and simultaneous, as befits our evening knowledge and infirmity of will.

The infirmity of the will is in effect a failure of attention in measuring the scale of nature against the standards of value. That is, our infirmity of will is the misalignment of our gaze from the Creator to the created, a failure to attend properly to the place of other created things in the order of nature. What is important is the quality of the will as it responds to the emotional disturbances that arise from within the soul itself. "For if the will is perverse, the emotions will be perverse; but if it is righteous, the emotions will be not only blameless, but praiseworthy." The emotions are, in fact, acts of will. Desire and joy are acts of will "in agreement with what we wish for." Fear and grief are acts of will "in disagreement with what we do not wish for." In this framework, the only thing we have to fear is sin itself—if our will is rightly aligned in loving good and hating evil, our emotions will be praiseworthy (CG 14.6, p. 590).

The will's four dispositions, then—desire and joy, fear and grief—depend upon both our capacity for attention and the objects to which we direct our attention. This struggle of attention manifests itself within the very experience of the human personality with respect to itself, in the tension between the flesh and the spirit. Augustine is at pains to emphasize that the body, as part of creation, is good. He disputes both Platonic and Manichean doctrines denigrating the body in favor of the soul. It cannot be the case, he says, that the soul is pure and the body evil, for such would be to disparage the creation that God saw and declared good (CG 14.5, pp. 588–90). Similarly, he disputes the Stoics' attempts to abolish emotions, and the Epicureans' insistence on maximizing pleasure and minimizing pain. The body and our emotions have their proper place, and are not to be dismissed or elevated unduly. In contrasting the flesh and spirit, Augustine follows scripture in assigning "flesh" to "the nature of man." The nature of the flesh is not evil, although to live "according to the flesh" is clearly an improper orientation of the will (CG 14.2, p. 582; CG 14.8, pp. 593ff).

The four dispositions of the will, then, are grounded in the two qualities of love. "When a man's purpose is to love God not according to man, but according to God, and to love his neighbor as himself, he is beyond doubt said to be of good will because of this love." What we call this love does not matter. *Caritas*, *amor*, *dilectio*, even *concupiscentia* are used in scripture, Augustine notes, to indicate good loves, and thus good wills. "A righteous will (*recta voluntas*), then, is a good love; and a perverted will (*voluntas perversa*) is an evil love" (CG 14.7, p. 592). The rightly turned will is good; the will turned around is evil. Emotions and affections which come from a love of the good are appropriate responses to "the infirmity of our human condition," the consequences of right reason; not to show emotion in the experience of this life would be unrighteous (CG 14.9, p. 599). To live according to the spirit and not according to the flesh is to love that which is immutable, and so to anchor acts of will "not with the anxiety of an infirmity which fears to sin, but with the tranquility of love" (CG 14.9, p. 601).

The interior landscape, then, culminates in an act of love oriented in obedience either to the law of the flesh or the law of God. These are the terms of the social landscape.

> Two cities, then, have been formed by two loves: that is, the earthly by love of self extending even to contempt of God, and the heavenly by love of God extending to contempt of self. The one, therefore, glories in itself, the other in the Lord; the one seeks glory from men, the other finds its highest glory in God, the Witness of our conscience. (CG 14.28, p. 632 reading *facio* as "formed" rather than "created")

The formation of the soul's loves finds its expression in the formation—the composition, framing—of the social world. The soul's loves, themselves, are expressions of value and of worship. *Contemptus/contemno* is the antonym of care (*carum esse*)—it means to devalue, to neglect, to consider inappropriately diminished. The English "contempt" does not fully capture the resonance of Augustine's framing—the contempt of God and of self is the misplacement of regard according to the standard of value set forth in the order of creation. The soul's loves are also expressions of the placement of glory—does one glory in oneself or in God? To glory is to praise, worship, laud, calling the question of the object of praise or worship. *Gloria* also shades to the appetite for glory, and hence for pride, calling the question of the worthiness of the object of glory.

The social term is city—*civitas*—the society of citizens. What binds them together? The order of their loves. The love of self is oriented inward and downward; it is private (*privatus*). The love of God is oriented outward, to neighbor, and upward, to God; it is public. And so Augustine contrasts that which is *privatus* with the things of the public, *res publica*. What does it mean to have a *civitas* formed by the love of the private? At the very least, the earthly city, formed by private loves, diminishes the human possibility.

> Adam and Eve would have been better fitted to resemble gods if they had clung in obedience to the highest and true ground of their being, and not, in their pride, made themselves their own ground. For created gods are gods not in their own true nature, but by participation in the true God. By striving after more, man is diminished; when he takes delight in his own self-sufficiency, he falls away from the One who truly suffices him. (CG 14.13, p. 610)

We are diminished by being our own ground. Our social order is diminished when it is formed by a grounding in what is privately created, rather than glorying in the creator.

What are the objects of care and glory? In misplacing our care and glory, in misaligning the things we value, we do harm to ourselves and others—we and others are diminished when we and they are not valued according to the order of creation. To measure things according to ourselves rather than to God is an act of pride, "an appetite for a perverse kind of elevation." *Perversio*: wrongly turned, inverted. To measure according to ourselves is to "forsake the foundation upon which the mind should rest, and to become and remain, as it were, one's own foundation" (CG 14.13, p. 608). The two competing social landscapes, then, are formed by humility and pride and are grounded respectively in God or in self.

The social poem is the realm of the fabulous—the fables and symbols which form our social imaginaries. For the earthly city, these fables and symbols express the story of human triumph, the inversion of the submission to the created order. For the heavenly city on earth, the fables are of humility, weakness, service to the Creator and created order. The earthly city is defined by mastery, but a false mastery. "It was because man forsook God by pleasing himself that he was handed over to himself, and, because he did not obey God, could not obey himself" (CG 14.24, p. 627).

These social poems express themselves on an historical stage, unfolding as it were in time their respective loves. The epic drama is the interweaving of the narratives of "two orders" which, "speaking allegorically," Augustine also calls "two cities," "two societies." The history of these two cities "extends throughout the whole of this time or age in which the dying pass away and the newly-born take their place" (CG 15.1, pp. 634, 635). The initial paradigmatic figures in this epic drama are Cain and Abel. Cain was born "a citizen of this world," while Abel was born "a pilgrim in this world, belonging to the City of God." Cain founded a city, whereas Abel, "a pilgrim, did not found one." Cain, the exile, wanders restlessly as a marked man, until he makes his own ground in founding a city. Abel's foundation is elsewhere. Echoing the two sons of Adam are the two sons of Abraham—"the one by a bondmaid, the other by a freewoman," born after "the flesh" and "by promise," respectively.

Augustine, following Paul, takes Ishmael and Isaac as two types of the city of Jerusalem. Ishmael is the citizen of the earthly

Jerusalem, bound by the law of Sinai; Isaac represents the freedom of the heavenly Jerusalem, the city of promise. The same city, two images—the earthly Jerusalem is an image of itself, established for its own sake; under the new covenant, however, this Jerusalem symbolizes something other than itself. Like Hagar and Ishmael, this Jerusalem is "the image of an image," a shadow which reveals the source of light precisely by its darkness. The earthly city "has two aspects," displaying both its own presence and pointing toward the heavenly city. Jerusalem is not the heavenly city on earth; but it is a negative space, as it were, which both highlights and points to that which it is not. It is a reminder of the epic drama of the heavenly city of humility which supervenes the earthly drama of proud mastery (CG 15.2, pp. 636, 637).

In the city of promise, "there is no love of a will that is personal and, so to speak, private, but a love that rejoices in a common and immutable good: a love, that is, that makes one heart out of many because it is the perfectly concordant obedience of charity" (CG 15.3, p. 638). *Ex multis unum cor faciens*: "making one heart out of many." What binds the city of promise is a unity of heart—con-cor-dia. By contrast, the earthly city is the region of dis-cord, "often divided against itself by lawsuits, wars and strife," by temporary victories which breed death, by the pride that presses it to seek victory over other nations. The goods sought by the earthly city are misplaced, but good nonetheless. The earthly city pursues war for the sake of peace, "albeit only for the sake of the lowest kinds of goods." When the higher goods are neglected, "and those other goods desired so much that they are thought to be the only goods, or loved more than the goods which are believed to be higher, then misery will of necessity follow, and present misery be increased by it" (CG 15.4, pp. 638, 639). The epic drama is the contest between the pursuit of higher and lower goods.

Unlike Jerusalem, the city of Rome, by contrast, has no double valence. It is the city of fratricide, of mastery, of tyranny. Romulus, overcome by envy, slays Remus, and so the very foundation of Rome is watered by blood. This is the drama that sings of arms and men. It is no wonder that the bloodied walls of Rome's founding unfold into the bloody wars of empire—the *mures* of violence yield the *mores* of war: an archetypal crime "mirrored by a kind of image of itself." Unlike Cain and Abel, who did not share the same desire for earthly things, Romulus and Remus sought a glory that only one could possess: "in order that one of them should wield entire mastery, his colleague was removed." The desire for earthly power and glory is zero sum. The desire for true goodness, by contrast, "is in no way lessened by the advent or continued presence of a sharer in it. On the contrary, goodness is a possession which is enjoyed more fully in proportion to the concord that exists between partners united in charity." These goods are not zero sum, but are possessed more abundantly "in proportion to the fullness with which he loves his partner in it" (CG 15.5, p. 640).

The earthly city is thus shown to be divided against itself in the contest of fleshly desire. The desire for the perfection of the flesh yields destruction in the contest for command in the mastery of others; the desire for the perfection of the spirit yields the unfolding of the potential of charity in the contest for self-mastery, self-command. The contrast, then, is of two narratives of the unfolding of individual and collective personality in the world: the narrative of the *mastery of* others and the narrative of *pilgrimage with* others. These two competing narratives both form and are formed by their corresponding social units over the course of time. The historical experiences of both communities are the same, but the existential responses of each are different.

The narrative of mastery is marked by trauma—the wounding of both victim and perpetrator: "the vessels of wrath." The narrative of pilgrimage is one of healing and, with healing, the possibilities of growth in love ushered in by forgiveness: "the vessels of mercy." When pilgrim travelers, through the punishment of sin, no longer yield to unrighteousness, "there is a change in us." Under God's rule, "man no longer conspires with himself to do evil. Rather, he finds, in his own changed mind, a gentler ruler here" (CG 15.6, p. 642).

The three pairs—Cain and Abel, Ishmael and Isaac, Romulus and Remus—are paradigmatic for the interweaving and contrasting desires of the earthly and heavenly cities. Abel is the pilgrim whose journey in time was ended abruptly. Cain is the fugitive who finds refuge not in heaven but in an earthly city of his own making. Isaac is the emblem of the heavenly Jerusalem pointed to by Ishmael's earthly Jerusalem. The Rome of Romulus and Remus points to nothing, save the civil war of a city divided against itself in pursuit of the mastery of finite earthly goods. Like Cain's city, Rome's peace is fugitive, a negative space of fleeting peace and restless loves. This negative space of fleeting peace is itself a good, but a qualified good—the bearer for a time of a material peace which nonetheless does not take part in the promise of spiritual rest. The earthly city which guarantees bodily security is, nonetheless, infertile ground for the nourishment of spiritual rest. Rome is not the bearer of Jerusalem's promise.

The epic poetry of history is the unfolding and interweaving of the narrative of relative material peace exercised through mastery and the narrative of spiritual promise exercised through the process of pilgrimage. Each epic journey is conducted under the aspect of two different notions of causality. The narrative of peace leans upon the structure of material and efficient causality, in which the means to the end (mastery) is mistaken for the end itself (peace). This confusion of means and ends is self-destructive and self-dividing. The narrative of promise leans upon the structures of formal and final causality, in which the ordering toward beauty is seen as the pilgrimage toward a fuller perfection of created potential.

The human artist is the master of external form—the imposition of form from without upon corporeal matter. This is what potters and painters do. The divine craftsman is the master of internal form, which is not attributable to any human action. This "internal kind of form" is a "divine and ... productive energy which cannot be made, but makes." The internal form, in turn, produces, "as their efficient cause," both corporeal forms and the very souls of living creatures; it "springs forth from the secret and hidden choice of a living and intelligent nature" (CG 12.26, p. 536). From the internal form arises, by means of the mystery of choice and action, both the efficient cause and the re-formation or de-formation of the internal formal cause. That is, our choices either refine the internal form toward its movement from limited to fuller perfection, or is destructive of the internal form in relation to its purpose.

Augustine is operating within Aristotle's framework of four causes. For Aristotle, all things may be described in terms of their material, formal, efficient, and final causes. The material cause is the matter, the stuff; the formal cause is the principle by which the matter is this shape rather than that; the efficient cause is the energy by which the matter is fashioned into this shape rather than that; and the final cause is the end or purpose for which the thing finds its proper shape and activity (Aristotle, *Metaphysics*, 1.983a and following). A knife may be made of metal and wood, but not just any blob of metal and wood constitutes a knife—this metal and wood take a particular form (within a range of variation) in order to be considered a knife. The efficient cause is the activity by which this metal and this wood is fashioned so as to become a knife. The final cause is the purpose of cutting (again within a range of variation), the end to which a knife is made or used. An excellent or virtuous knife (the Greek *arête* means both excellence and virtue) is one of superior materials fashioned according to a superior form, and which serves its purpose in a superior manner. We may see an analogy to the relation of individual and species: chef's knives, paring knives, boning knives, pocket knives all have similar and distinct kinds of excellence.

So too with the being of all created beings, and with our souls, for Augustine. To speak of the material cause of the soul is perhaps a little jarring, but Augustine is clear that creation comprises both material and spiritual nature. The fact that we cannot touch the soul (or the angels) does not entail—logically or actually—the elimination of the notion of the material cause. If we are to say (however metaphorically) that the soul has a substance and a shape, we are operating with the categories of material and formal causality. By his own account, one of Augustine's most profound intellectual conversions is the realization that God does not have a body. This imaginative shift to the possibility of spiritual as well as material realities, inspired by his reading of the Platonists, allowed Augustine to separate himself from the thoroughgoing materialism of the Manichees, as well as from the materialism of the Epicureans and, in a qualified sense, the materialism of the Stoics as well (CF 3.7, pp. 60ff).

Augustine places the Aristotelian framework of causality within his own, teleological framework of measure, number, and weight. Just as in Aristotelian and Newtonian physics there is a natural resting place or equilibrium of motion, so too there is a gravitational pull on our soul to find its rest. This resting place is encoded, as it were, in the internal form; it is jostled from its rest by the repeated impositions of efficient causes which resist or contradict its rest in measure, number, and weight. Either the formal cause produces efficient causes which are properly the unfolding of the latent measure, number, and weight (this is the natural movement of the divine energy), or our efficient causes interfere with and distort the natural movement of the divine energy, folding the soul in on itself.

This interference and distortion Augustine refers to as a "deficient cause," that is, a failure or mis-orientation of the efficient cause which results in a deformation of the soul. In its deficiency, the will resists its resting place, defects from "that which supremely is" in favor of that which has "a less perfect degree of being." Augustine is clear that the defections of the will are not toward things which are evil by nature or in themselves, but defections against the order of nature, giving undue (and therefore unjust) attention to the ordering of created goods (CG 12.7-9, pp. 507–11). This inversion of the order of goods is "a defective movement [*defectivus motus*]," a corruption of form, a distortion of measure, number, and weight (FW 2.20.203-204, p. 83).

The two poems of nature and history reflect two orders—one vertical, one horizontal. To act in history is to occupy the intersection of the order of nature and the order of history. How one acts in history reflects how one views one's place in the order of nature. Unlike other animals, humans have a substantial capacity to enact, or not, the order of nature—it is part of our nature to have the capacity to choose whether or not to obey the order of nature. Put another way, we can act in history so as to disrupt or enhance the harmony of created nature.

Together, the two poems of nature and history, of the vertical and the horizontal, are the poems of authority and freedom. History unfolds in the panoply of possibility limited by the rational seeds implanted in all created things, and in the imaginative choices of human reason. To act is to be an actor—to have authority (*auctor* < *auctoritas*) in the disposition of one's choice. In the order of history, our authority is limited only by power; in the order of nature, our authority is limited by the voluntary obedience to the scale of value inherent in created nature. We have authority over a wide but proper sphere; and we are subject to the higher authority of the laws of nature—physical and moral—and their divine origin.

To possess, exercise, and be subject to authority is also to participate in an order of causality. The sin of pride is the mistaken assertion of unlimited power in the place of limited authority—it is to step outside the proper sphere of action. The order of nature is the sphere of formal and final causality, which limits authority and action by ordering them to the beauty of the created order. The order of history is the sphere of material and efficient causality, which manifests authority and action in terms of power. Absent the scale of meaning and value inherent in the order of nature, action becomes merely the exercise of power—the matrix of causality is collapsed into the manipulation of matter, i.e., raw force.

To be authorities subject only to the laws of our own making is to neglect the poem of nature, to collapse the vertical order of measure, number, and weight into the horizontal line of history. It flattens our existence by removing the scale of value and subjecting created beings only to material and efficient causality in time. The freedom of the order of history resolves itself into mere force in the absence of the dynamic tension of the order of nature and the limits it places on power. The order of nature, without the possibility of unfolding in time, remains static, with no opportunities for learning or creative unfolding.

The intersection, then, of the order of nature and the order of history creates a dynamic tension in which all created beings are allowed to unfold their inherent potential. Human beings in particular, by virtue of reason, can unfold that potential in the fullness of causality, or not. Non-human animals by their very nature live fully according to their measure, number, and weight, oriented necessarily to the fourfold causality: material, formal, efficient, and final. That is, non-human animals are not susceptible to deficient causality—they cannot choose not to live formally and teleologically. Humans, by contrast, can choose to live contrary to the formal and final dimensions of their created being. In so doing, humans also interfere with the formal and final causes of other beings in created nature.

What does it mean to be an actor who acts against the good of his own nature? In usurping authority not granted by God in the order of nature, human beings introduce a fifth dimension of causality. Augustine calls this a deficient cause (*causa deficiens*). An efficient cause properly provides the energy for conforming matter (including spirit) to its formal and final condition. A deficient cause disorients its energy to the deformation of matter and spirit in pursuit of secondary ends.

To know our place in history we need to know our place in the order of nature. To grow and learn in the order of nature we need to find our place in the order of history. This dynamic tension is the condition of growth and learning toward the greater perfection for which we were created. The expansion of our measure, number, and weight takes place within that dynamic tension. When that tension is collapsed, our measure, number, and weight are likewise contracted.

What are we to make, then, of an age which has collapsed the order of nature to the order of history? This folding of nature onto history hampers the unfolding of our measure, number, and weight. Ours is an age which prizes material and efficient causality, subordinating formal and final causality to the point that they are forgotten altogether. Measure, number, and weight lose their ontological dimensionality and are resolved into quantifiable matter alone—the three-dimensional qualities of being are neglected altogether.

Augustine would call our world a world of excessively deficient causality, one which has withdrawn from the qualitative scale of value which honors formal and final causality in favor of a quantitative scale which has no reference but itself and conceives all relations in terms of the Newtonian mechanics of efficient causality. This quantitative, mechanistic view of causality (and thus of value) is in fact arbitrary. Absent an order of formal and final cause, there is no reason for energy to be directed in one way rather than another. In such a world, we are subject to the laws of power alone. What does this mean for the conception of law? Within the tension of the order of nature and the order of history, law is oriented toward emergent beauty. Within the order of history alone, law is ordered toward force.

Empire is out of place; it expands beyond its limits in impropriety, trampling the physical and moral landscape of created nature. Cain is the exile who must make his own home in the city. Abel is the pilgrim who finds his home in created nature. The exile considers nature a threat, an imposition. The pilgrim looks to nature as a teacher and a judge. These opposite dispositions entail an attitude toward law. For the exile, the law condemns; for the pilgrim, the law gives life. These opposite dispositions also entail contrasting attitudes toward progress. For the exile, progress is found in the conquest of space, the mastery of matter. The pilgrim, by contrast, flourishes in the gift of time, the mastery of self by grace, which gives life. The exile, who is not at home in the scale of value of created nature, sees his journey as a ladder or railway traversing space in the acts of forceful acquisition. The pilgrim, whose gaze is oriented in the scale of value of created nature, conceives progress as formation and re-formation in the qualities of being rather than having; his activity is not marked by material expansion, but by spiritual expansion, the expansion of love beyond desire.

The exile lives in illusion measured by quantity; the pilgrim journeys in mystery measured by quality. For the exile, limits are obstacles to be overcome by force. For the pilgrim, limits are places of mystery where love can flourish. The threefold drama of action, then, is a contest between the poem of love and the poem of force. Created nature pulls force toward the elegance of love; history strives to overcome love with the ugliness of force. This contest occurs within the human heart, within the social order, and over time. The paradox of the mosaic of action is that for us to know our soul's home, we step outside of ourselves. To come to know our place in the social order, we must step outside of the city. To know our place in history, we must step into the stream of timelessness. Having stood outside, having embraced *ex-stasis*, we must then step back in.

What is self-referential is necessarily arbitrary. Power and history are self-referential unless they are referred to nature. What is true for Gödel in mathematics is true also in the moral realm—a system can only be valued from outside itself—the poem of history only has meaning when referred to the order of nature. Beauty requires the relationship of parts and whole, not the abstract diminution of parts and wholes when parts are separated from the whole. These relationships are personal at the center and mysterious at the limit because they cannot be reduced or specialized to the individual apart from the whole, nor can they ever be fully explained. The mysterious is not only the vector of humility (in knowledge) but also the condition of continued curiosity and learning.

History, no less than creation, reads us. History and the soul mirror each other—the interior landscape of the human soul in time writes itself on the parchment of history. To act in history is, then, a valuation between the love of beauty and the love of force. The former is the unfolding of nature, the latter a deformation of the created order. The events of history provide the matter, as it were, of action, but the scale of value of nature provides meaning. Without the poem of nature, the poem of history is merely a string of random events. Without the poem of history, the poem of nature lacks dimensionality or texture. The ever-creative action of calibrating the horizontal with the vertical is the interweaving of the two poems in the fabric of the law—the law of the heart and the law of the city.

3

Righteousness Unbound

If nature and history are poems to be read together, justice is a song to be composed and sung. Both Plato and Aristotle speak of justice in the city in musical terms, but Cicero is Augustine's more immediate interlocutor. In *The City of God*, Augustine quotes Cicero's *On the Republic* at length:

> Among the different sounds of lyres or flutes and the voices of singers, a certain harmony must be maintained which the cultivated ear cannot bear to hear disrupted or discordant; and such harmony, concordant and consistent, may be brought about by the balancing of even the most dissimilar voices. So too, when the highest, lowest and, between them, the intermediate orders of society are balanced by reason as though they were voices, the city may embody a consonance blended of quite dissimilar elements. What musicians call harmony in singing is concord in the city, which is the most artful and best bond of security in the commonwealth, and which, without justice, cannot be secured at all. (CG 2.21, p. 77)

How are parts to be arranged in a whole free of discord? Reason balances disparate voices in a concordant, consistent harmony, the essential component of which is justice. Each voice must be given its due—it must sing its distinctive song, but for the good of the whole song each voice, each instrument must also be modulated, moderated in view of the song as a whole.

Cicero's *Republic* is a dialogue, and the passage Augustine cites and discusses engages this debate: does the bringing of harmony to the disparate voices of the city require the imposition of injustice or the rule of supreme justice? That is, does the modulation of voices require that injustice be done, or that there be a principle by which justice can be done to all? Does the imposition of justice require the violation of an individual voice's nature? In Cicero's dialogue, Cicero's Scipio takes the latter position, which is the focus of Augustine's treatment. But the form of the argument—both Cicero's and Augustine's—must remain fully in view. The terms of the discussion are fundamentally aesthetic—the aim is the beauty of harmony. The standard for what is true about justice is what is beautiful to the moral ear.

What constitutes a beautifully formed people? Augustine cites Cicero-Scipio: "A 'people' he defines as being not every assembly or multitude, but an assembly united in fellowship by common agreement as to what is right (*ius*) and by a community of interest (*utilitas*)." A people is only a people to the degree that is has *ius* and *utilitas* in common. What sustains a people, according to Cicero, is the combination of "ancient ways" (traditions and institutions) and "excellent men" (examples) in mutual support of one another (*veterem morem ac maiorum instituta retinebant excellentes viri*). Cicero goes on to describe his own age as a faded painting—in the absence of excellent men, Rome has neglected to restore the republic's former colors or to preserve the vestige of the image it inherited, or even to reinforce the image's defining lines.

If justice is a story, a people is a painting whose lines and colors must constantly be refreshed. The painting has a symbolic force, both as a reflection of the people and as the image that binds them together as an object of striving. The painting, faded or otherwise, is at once reflective-descriptive and normative. It is sustained and restored only by the *mores* of the most exemplary among a people.

Augustine, in this passage, is interested in definitions, and promises to argue that Rome never was a republic because "true justice was never present in it." But his attention is further directed to the degree to which Rome or any other city is worthy of praise. The words of Psalm 87:3: "Glorious things are spoken of thee, O City of God" highlights Augustine's conclusion that "True justice, however, does not exist other than in that commonwealth whose Founder and Ruler is Christ" (CG 2.21, p. 80).

When, in Book 19, Augustine returns to Cicero's definition of a commonwealth, his challenge is to find a definition which is both normative and descriptive. On the one hand, the challenge is logical—if justice is elusive, so too is a commonwealth properly so called. "No true justice, no true commonwealth" is a difficult analytical formulation on which to build a political science. On the other hand, Augustine's challenge is more fundamental: in identifying "a people," how does one distinguish between an association and mere multitude? That is, what makes a collectivity a society rather than simply an aggregation of individuals?

With Cicero, Augustine rejects the definition that justice is the interest of the stronger in favor of "justice is that virtue which gives to each his due" (CG 19.21, pp. 950, 951; cf. FW 1.13.90). True justice entails service of the one true God—we must give God His due. But the definition leaves Augustine in the same predicament— in a world conditioned by original sin, there can be no true worship of God and therefore no justice and no commonwealth (CG 19.21, pp. 951, 952).

Even as he shifts definitions, Augustine retains Cicero's framework—a people remains a song, the city remains a painting. What is it that provides the sweet harmonies, the defined lines, the vibrant colors? The whole of *City of God* Book 19 is a meditation on the classical virtues, so it is not a surprise that Augustine is trying to situate justice, as well as temperance, fortitude, and prudence within the scale of value of created nature. "Nothing is 'in the interest' of those who live godlessly"—that is, those who have separated themselves from their measure, number, and weight. Virtues are not virtues at all, Augustine maintains, unless they are referred to God (CG 19.21, p. 952; CG 19.25, p. 961).

Interest, *utilitas*, what is beneficial—Augustine redefines utility not in relation to self alone but in doing justice to God and to neighbor—that is, to love them according to their place in the order of creation: God as creator, neighbor as creature, human neighbor as creature made in God's image. Right (*ius*) springs from justice (*iustitia*) and justice derives from love. This shift of register allows Augustine to adduce a new definition of a people with a different vocabulary altogether: "a 'people' is an assembled multitude of rational creatures bound together by a common agreement as to the objects of their love." A people, we might paraphrase, is an assembly of creatures using their reason to understand their linkages to the whole by virtue of their creation and by conventions of their own design. This definition is adequate to the descriptive task: "if we are to discover the character of any people, we have only to examine what it loves." Any assemblage of rational creatures may be called a people regardless of the objects of its loves. The definition is also adequate to the normative task: "Clearly, however, the better the objects of the agreement, the better the people, and the worse the objects, the worse the people" (CG 19.24, p. 960).

Aristotle, in the *Politics*, maintains that all communities aim at some good, which is to say, at what they think to be good. His definition too meets the demands of both the descriptive and the normative while raising, like Augustine, the fundamental question: what is the good for the community? and what is the good for me? For Aristotle, the *polis* is the highest and best form of community— the logical and moral end to which other forms of community (household, village, tribe) are directed. "Justice is the bond of men in cities," writes Aristotle, and Cicero follows his lead. Augustine does too, but with an added dimension: the love of justice binds a people together, but justice can only be realized through love of God and neighbor according to the scale of created nature.

Justice, in Augustine's framework, is not, then, the assertion of rights but rather the honoring of the responsibilities of love rooted in our very createdness. Augustine retains Cicero's aesthetic framework—he folds it into his own normative structure of created order—even as he shifts the terms of the definition of what it means to be a people. The criterion remains concord, "the bond of concord ... is, as it were, the health of a people" (CG 19.24, p. 960). A people's song and a city's painting is animated by its concord, which in turn is infused with the quality of its loves.

Concord has an emotional resonance—literally con-cordia is the joining of hearts. But its basis is not primarily that of sentiment. A people is an assemblage of rational creatures—reason opens more widely to embrace the love of God and neighbor as an expression of the rational apprehension of one's place in the scale of nature, and therefore of one's responsibilities within the order of created nature. Gratitude is rational, a fullness of mind and heart in conjunction— so much so that even the more narrowly rationalistic Hobbes calls ingratitude the unforgiveable sin. Concord has its basis not in the reconciliation of aggregated competing rights, but in the rational ordering of mutual responsibilities referred to an understanding of a good life measure by the order of nature.

Social life is a song or painting, then, which is formed by the poems of nature and history. By nature (Augustine is citing Varro), we desire four things: pleasure, rest, a combination of the two, and "the primary objects of nature," viz., bodily safety and mental integrity (CG 19.1, p. 910). History supplies the traditions and institutions which form a peoples' *mores*. By nature, we desire virtue; by history, we learn virtue, which Augustine calls "the art of living." Social life, then, is both the painted and the painter, the song and the singer. The art of living, necessarily in ensemble, is thus an unrehearsed virtuosic performance, an experiment and improvisation—individually and collectively in social life—in which our conception of the final good shapes and is shaped by the way of life by which we pursue it. Social life is both the locus of self-awareness and the space of learning to correct our conduct (CG 19.3, pp. 916, 917). In short, social life is the studio or recital hall of virtue.

While virtue "is the most excellent of all the goods of the soul," it aims at the good use of the goods of body and soul conjointly. Virtue, now personified in Augustine's discussion, enacts the same reflexivity of the pursuit of the good: "she herself desires all these objects [of body and soul] for their own sake, and at the same time seeks her own increase also. Thus she makes use of them and of herself simultaneously, so that she may delight in all of them and enjoy them all" (CG 19.3, pp. 916, 917).

Not every kind of life is virtue, "but only a wisely conducted life" comprising memory and reason (the preconditions of any teaching or learning) and fellowship. Fellowship Augustine defines rather broadly, in keeping with his account of creation. There can be no doubt that "this happy life is a social one: that is it loves the good of friends as much as its own, and for their sake wishes for them what it wishes for itself." These friends, broadly construed, range from: family, city, human society across nations, to "the universe itself, which we call heaven and earth, and to those whom the philosophers call gods, whom they hold to be a wise man's friends." These concentric circles of friendship loosely construed constitute the field of sociability in which we learn the art of living, by which Augustine means the art of living well. And while Augustine addresses only rational creatures, to the extent that we wish for the non-rational creatures of the universe what we have—existence—there is an opening to the notion that we learn the art of living well also in relation to the continued existence of other species. Just as Darwin will later maintain that the human species will learn to extend compassion beyond family, tribe, nation, and species to embrace other species, Augustine's account of creation enjoins human virtue to respect the measure, number, and weight of all non-human creatures.

In the structure of Augustine's thinking, nature and history are momentarily subsumed within the order of social life. As we learn from our range of friends, we also desire what is good for them as well as ourselves. Or rather, we learn to see that our own good is implicated in the good of the range of friends around us. This, then, is the bond of responsibility for which, in Augustine's thinking, our modern notion of rights would be a solvent. To assert a right is to utter a demand. Responsibility—*responsum*—is an answer, a promise, an agreement with respect to the call of justice—to render unto each which is due in the spirit of friendship.

If social life is the studio or recital hall of virtue, it is not a realm of failsafe institutions. On the contrary, social life is rife with ills, the clash of compound infirmities: the internal warfare of flesh and spirit writ large in the "injuries, suspicions, hostilities and war" of human affairs. There is treachery in the family, conflict in the city, and peoples are divided by language, which impedes their mutual understanding. Even the universe deceives us—Augustine speaks in terms of the deceptions of demons, but we may draw a more philosophical conclusion derived from his angelology (CG 19.4, p. 921; 19.5, p. 925; CG 19.9, p. 931). Simply, things are not in reality what we perceive them to be.

None of the concentric circles of friendship is immune from strife. To this uncertainty is added ignorance—of the motivations of actions of others, of contingent facts, of our own internal desires. We deceive ourselves. The famous passage at *City of God* 19.6 is but a special, exemplary case of the more general predicament of making decisions in conditions of infirmity and ignorance. A judge in a court of law "can never penetrate the consciousness" of those upon whom he passes judgment. The torture of witnesses for testimony, permitted by Roman law, is unreliable, as is the difficulty of actually proving the truth of one's accusations. And yet, the judge must decide. "On the one hand, ignorance is unavoidable, and, on the other, judgment is also unavoidable because human sociability compels it" (CG 19.6, p. 927 modifying "human society" to "human sociability"). Augustine's judge is a special case which illustrates the kinds of decisions we all must make; in responding to the responsibilities inherent in human sociability, we judge—much the way a painter or a singer judges the stroke of the brush or the color of a note.

Even in the most controlled of circumstances, human judgment occurs in conditions of frailty and uncertainty. But the logic of Augustine's argument is to emphasize that, by virtue of participating in social life, we are all judges, whether we sit in a court of law or not. We do not always know the truth about others, our circumstances, or ourselves. We may not rightly see the arguments of truth adduced by others, or see through the falsehoods of those who would deceive us. Amid the shadows of social life, as Augustine observes, we are nonetheless called to take our seat on the bench of judgment, "for the claims of human society, which he thinks it wicked to abandon, constrain him and draw him to this duty" (CG 19.6, p. 927). The pain of our duty toward others is a greater good than the comforts of avoiding judgment altogether. The misery of this predicament is to be acknowledged with compassion. The exercise of duty toward others may interfere with the feelings of happiness, but recognizing the necessity of sacrificing one's own happiness in living responsibly toward others is "more worthy of the dignity of man" (CG 19.6, p. 928). It may be our lot to judge, but it is also our dignity.

The realm of law is thus fraught with uncertainty, but in the drama of duty in social life, a dignity emerges which has its own tragic beauty. Just as there is violence in the order of nature, so the painting of social life has regions of shadow; singing the song of social life is not immune from the minor keys.

In stark contrast with the judge who sacrifices his own happiness in service to social life, Augustine adduces the mythical monster Cacus, who lives a solitary life in a cave—without friends, without family, without the warmth of human sociability. He gives nothing to anyone, and takes whatever he wants from others with violence (CG 19.12, p. 935). Unlike war and bands of robbers—forms of violence which necessarily entail limited or misdirected sociability—Cacus represents the extreme of a-sociability (one recalls Aristotle's statement that a man without a city is either a beast or a god). Both Cacus and the long-suffering judge live in misery, but the virtues of the judge's miseries are laid bare when juxtaposed with those of Cacus. Again one thinks of Aristotle, for whom we become more fully human through the act of discussing and deciding matters of justice in the city.

Cacus is the epitome of exile, even to his physical separation from the city. But he is an emblem of the selfish a-sociability within the city—an exile who seeks his own alone, the private, in the love and assertion of self. The long-suffering judge is the epitome of pilgrimage, making "good use of the ills which a man suffers," to turn the ills of social life into the blessings of peace, such as they can be achieved (CG 19.10, p. 932). In this sense, the pilgrim is the greatest friend of the city, one whose attachments are well ordered and who wants to use the things of this world not to wrest them away, but to leave them in their proper place.

Both Cacus and the longsuffering judge seek peace, but by different means and of a different quality. Cacus's peace, the peace of exile, is partial; he is not imposed upon by others—he has power and autonomy but no love. We see in him the deformation of created nature, not its approximation of perfection. Peace pursued in sociability is more comprehensive, not simply as the absence of being victimized, but in the positive development of a better nature. Peace, then, not happiness, is our Final Good, according to Augustine, where peace is understood as a higher concord, sometimes despite and sometimes because of the ills of this world. The order of nature and the order of history find their consummation in the provisional peace of social life, which is both the workshop of virtue and its expression. Our happiness is in proportion to the degree that our moral peace approximates the peace of the heavenly Jerusalem, the "Vision of Peace" (CG 19.11, pp. 932, 933).

The motions of the will and the classical virtues are thus subsumed under the desire for peace. Desire and joy, fear and grief strive for peace or seek to disrupt it. Virtue personified aims to use justice, temperance, fortitude, and prudence—to use the art of living itself—in pursuit of peace. The laws of nature are the laws of peace, whether in the world of wild animals or in the social world of human beings.

> What tigress does not purr softly over her cubs and lay her fierceness aside while she caresses them? ... How much more strongly, then, is a man drawn by the laws of his nature, so to speak, to enter into a similarly peaceful association with his fellow men, so far as it lies within his power to do so? (CG 19.12, p. 936)

Pride expressed through dominion is the misdirected means toward a legitimate end, a substitution of efficient causality for formal causality. Humility is that obedience to formal causality which does not seek to impose a peace of its own making, but rather to conform to the order of the laws of peace which lie beyond it. "Pride is the perverted imitation of God. For pride hates a fellowship of equality under God, and wishes to impose its own dominion upon its equals, in place of God's rule. Therefore it hates the just peace of God, and it loves its own unjust peace, but it cannot help loving peace of some kind or another" (CG 19.12, p. 936).

Pride, the rejection of the law of God's order, is a rejection of the fellowship of equality of God's order. And yet, God's order is hierarchical. The unjust peace which erodes the ordered hierarchy of nature in the name of equality in fact dissolves the fellowship of equality in favor of dominion. The spirit of right without the spirit of responsibility leads to the love of dominion, replacing the free obedience to God with the imposed obedience to man. The spirit of responsibility yields a sense of duty and service in a fellowship of equality under God. Augustine's claim is paradoxical; only in conditions of natural and social hierarchy are a just peace and fellowship of equality realized.

The natural law of peace can never be wholly usurped—even the love of an unjust peace is still peace, however fragmentary and deformed: "Even that which is perverse, however, must of necessity be in, or derived from, or associated with, and to that extent at peace with, some part of the order of things among which it has its being or of which is consists. Otherwise, it would not exist at all" (CG 19.12, p. 936). An unjust peace is a failure of form.

The absence of peace, then, is like the absence of good—for Augustine (as for Plato) nothing can be wholly evil, for to exist is to possess some good. Evil is not an independent substance but the absence of good. In this sense, the structure of Augustine's thinking about peace is the aesthetic-moral analog to his ontological-moral account of the good. To exist is to participate in and love some form of peace (CG 19.13, p. 939).

The love of an unjust peace takes on its own inertia: we become accustomed to our condition of dissonance, and yet some intimation of the harmony of the order reminds us both of the tranquility we possess and the greater tranquility which we have lost and not yet regained. Pain is our resistance to the tranquility of order, and it is by "the law of order" that we are justly severed from the blessings of peace. In resisting the tranquility of order we, in effect, punish ourselves. When we persist in our resistance, we become accustomed to the self-inflicted misery of our punishment and are habituated to deformed arts of living (CG 19.13, pp. 938, 939). Cacus's wretchedness is self-inflicted, and yet his wretchedness and existence presuppose that he still participates in enough peace to know that he is miserable in the peace he loves. The judge, by contrast, takes solace in his tragic misery in the faith that his action aims at a more just peace. The way of the exile and the way of the pilgrim view the law of order in very different colors.

Resistance to the order of nature is thus a disturbance in the tranquility of order, a deformation of the law of peace which ripples through the fabric of nature, history, and social life. The lyric, the epic, and the fabulous are intertwined and expressed in the law of peace. This is the context of Augustine's famous definition of peace. What in English is a series of tightly wrought sentences is, in Augustine's Latin, a prolonged melodic line which must be quoted in full:

> The peace of the body, therefore, lies in the balanced ordering of its parts; the peace of the irrational soul lies in the rightly ordered disposition of the appetites; the peace of the rational soul lies in the rightly ordered relationship of cognition and action; the peace of body and soul lies in the rightly ordered life and health of a living creature; peace between mortal man and God is an ordered obedience, in faith, under an eternal law; and peace between men is an ordered agreement of mind with mind. The peace of the household is an ordered concord, with respect to command and obedience, of those who dwell together; the peace of a city is an ordered concord, with respect to command and obedience, of the citizens; and the peace of the Heavenly City is a perfectly ordered and perfectly harmonious fellowship in the enjoyment of God, and of one another in God. The peace of all things lies in the tranquillity of order; and order is the disposition of equal and unequal things in such a way as to give to each its proper place. (CG 19.13, p. 938)

The picture Augustine paints in words can be visualized as a complex mosaic:

Ontology	Terminology	Type of Peace	Description
Physical	Material	1. Body	Harmony of physical parts
	Immaterial	2. Irrational soul	Harmony of appetites
	Willful	3. Rational soul	Harmony of knowledge and action
Spiritual	Love of self	4. Body and soul	Harmony of life and health
	Love of God	5. Man and God	Obedience to eternal law
	Love of neighbor	6. Man and man	Well ordered concord
Social	*Pax domus*	7. Domestic peace	Concord of ruling and obedience of family
	Pax civitatis (nb: not *civitas terrena*)	8. Civil peace	Concord of ruling and obedience of citizens
	Pax caelestis civitatis	9. Heavenly peace	Most perfectly ordered concord of enjoyment of God and one another in God

The law of peace is not a doctrine of aggregated rights, but the disposition of parts in a coherent whole. We must imagine what is often called Augustine's catalogue of peace not as a table but as an arch illustrating the symmetry of physical harmony and social concord completed by spiritual obedience.

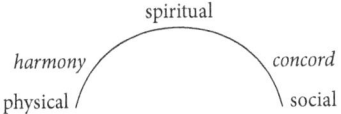

The love of God sits atop the arch of peace as a capstone which holds the structure of natural and social tranquility together. The peace of the order of nature is described in terms of harmony. The order of social life is described in terms of concord. Both harmony and concord give way at the top to a love of God expressed as (willing, voluntary) obedience to eternal law. In both the natural order and the social order there is relative inequality with respect to natural and conventional hierarchy, but absolute equality before God. Between man and God there can be no equality because there is a fundamental difference in kind between creature and creator. That is, there can be no concord, no unity of heart—rather, there is a unifying love which transcends the difference in kind; it is a categorically different form of the unity of heart. In the love of neighbor there is concord but no obedience. By contrast, the domestic peace and civil peace are conditions of concord described in terms of command and obedience—among those who live together and those who are fellow citizens. If we follow the symmetrical structure, the city would seem to be the locus of command and obedience with respect to the harmony of rational appetites; the household the realm of command and obedience with respect to the harmony of rational knowledge and action; love of neighbor is a concord not founded in command and obedience but in parallel to the harmony of life and health characteristic of the love of self. In all, natural harmony and social concord support the triangle of the great commandments to love God and to love neighbor as one's self (CG 19.14, p. 941).

Through the center of the arch is, as it were, the linear progression of history, both individual and collective. In addition to the symmetrical logic of the catalog of peace, there is a linear logic—the harmony or integrity of the physical and spiritual in the individual reflects and supports the love of self and love of God, which in turn is the basis of the love of neighbor, of family, of city, and ultimately the peace of the heavenly city. Harmony and concord—forms of relationship which are not formed by command and obedience—are to inform those orders (household and city) where order is necessarily formed by command and obedience, yielding in heaven a perfectly ordered concord in which relationships of command and obedience pass away. The language of *ius* and *iustitia* has given way to the language of peace—the arc of history bends, as it were, toward peace.

The symmetry of the arch of peace underscores the joint and parallel necessity of physical and social tranquility. That is, for

Augustine, social tranquility is not a luxury to be fulfilled after the physical needs are met, nor can social tranquility be enjoyed in the absence of the satisfaction of basic physical needs. Rather, the physical and social needs are jointly basic in support of a healthy material-spiritual existence. Social tranquility may follow from physical tranquility in time, but not in the logic of significance. The human person is body and soul, and the integrity (in the sense of wholeness) of each is dependent equally on physical and social tranquility.

Physical and social tranquility are goods which may be used well or ill. When used well, directed toward the love of God, both earthy and heavenly peace are enjoyed: "He who uses temporal goods ill, however, shall lose them, and shall not receive eternal goods either" (CG 19.13, p. 940). Only when temporal physical and social goods are pursued for eternal, spiritual ends are they enjoyed in their fullness.

The symmetry of the arch of peace also helps structure our understanding of the relation among physical and social organizations. The love of God orders, as final cause, the material, immaterial, and willful in the harmony of life and health that constitutes the love of self. That is, the physical is drawn upward, as it were, by the spiritual as final cause. But the love of God also cascades downward, as it were, as formal cause, giving spiritual order to physical phenomena. So too in the relations among social organizations. The love of God orders, as final cause, heavenly, civil, and domestic society toward the well-ordered concord which constitutes the love of neighbor. The social is drawn upward, toward love of neighbor, by the spiritual as final cause. Similarly, the love of God cascades downward, as it were, as formal cause.

The relations among social organizations have long vexed readers of Augustine because (modern) readers are inclined to see those relations through the lens of efficient causality, rather than in terms of the dynamic interplay between formal and final causality. The penultimate concord in the order of final causality is the love of neighbor—the city and the household find their fulfillment in the love of neighbor. Relations of command and obedience cease in the concord of mutual love in which self and God are ordinately loved. Inversely, love of neighbor forms, in lesser approximations, the concord among members of a household and among citizens. The love of neighbor properly forms, or informs—manifests itself—to a lesser degree, in the household and the city. Put another way, the household and the city are properly forms of the expression of the love of neighbor. Domestic and civic relationships of command and obedience are thus both formed by and directed toward a concord which is not characterized by command and obedience. Heavenly redemption is the spiritual and chronological parallel to creation, viewed not as a return to the original spiritual society at creation (at the beginning of time), but to the greater perfection of spiritual society in heaven (at the end of time).

In the order of final causality, the city and the household are the progressive conditions under which we come to learn (logically, not chronologically) the virtues which manifest the concord which is the love of neighbor. Our civic obligations of command and obedience are weaker than our domestic obligations—the form of the love intensifies as we move from civil to domestic to neighborly sociability and the experience of command and obedience is less involuntary—until obedience is altogether, in love of neighbor, a response to an internal rather than external command. Chronologically, of course, we experience the command and obedience of the household first, and tend to delight in the weakening of bonds that comes with civil association. The movement is not so much from involuntary to voluntary, but from external to internal authority and obedience—we learn in the city and household the habits of virtue that find their fulfillment in the concord of neighborly love. Similarly, in the order of formal causality, we bring the experience of neighborly love to the relationship of command and obedience which characterizes the household and the city.

The cascade of neighborly love downward Augustine discusses in terms of the duties of care. In obeying the command to love our neighbors as ourselves, we also wish our neighbor to do the same for us. Neighborly love is, thus, both a gift given and a gift received. In loving one's neighbor, one wishes to be loved in return in ways that help me love myself and God more fully. This is the structure of mutual care.

The "order of concord," according to Augustine, "is, first, that a man should harm no one, and, second, that he should do good to all, so far as he can" (CG 19.14, p. 941). This moral counterpart to the Hippocratic Oath begins with self-restraint—don't sin against others or be occasions for their sin—and continues with action—be a conduit of final causality toward the love of God and of formal causality toward the love of neighbor. Our duty extends further: we do harm to others when we neglect to restrain them from sin or fail to punish them for their sin, both as correction and as an example to others (CG 19.16, p. 945).

The order of responsibility is practically determined by nature and social proximity. We begin by caring for our own household, "for the order of nature and of human society itself gives him readier access to them, and greater opportunity of caring for them." The care of the household is "the foundation of domestic peace," a concord which derives from the spirit of pilgrimage.

> In the household of the just man, however, who "lives by faith" and who is still a pilgrim on his way to that Heavenly City, even those who command are the servants of those whom they seem to command. For it is not out of any desire for mastery that they command; rather, they do so from a dutiful concern for others (*sed officio consulendi*): not out of pride in ruling, but because they love mercy. (CG 19.14, p. 942)

Command is hierarchical; just command is not oppressive. Augustine's key word here is *consulo*: to consider, deliberate, to take care of or be mindful of, to have regard for. There is a further political resonance to a Roman ear, which understands the role of the republican consul as *primus inter pares* charged with the temporary administration of the common good, in contrast with the individually and politically self-aggrandizing rule of the *imperator*, who does not see his office as temporary. The just man commands with the spirit of the consul, exercising the demands of a temporary office for the good of the whole, not a permanent office for the good of one.

"For it is not out of any desire for mastery that they command; rather, they do so from a dutiful concern for others: not out of pride in ruling, but because they love mercy." The structure of Augustine's beautifully compact sentence is illuminating, shifting the weight of command from mastery to service. Desire (*cupiditas*) gives way to duty (*officium*); mastery (*dominandi*) yields to thoughtful regard (*consulendi*); ruling (*principandi*) relinquishes itself in the act of providing, with an eye to the future (*providendi*); and pride (*superbia*) is abandoned in favor of kindheartedness (*misericordia*).

Tyranny	→	Command
cupiditas (desire)	→	*officium* (duty of service)
dominandi (mastery)	→	*consulendi* (thoughtful regard)
principandi (ruling)	→	*providendi* (providing for the future)
superbia (pride)	→	*misericordia* (kindheartedness)

The order of nature, Augustine continues, gives man—God's rational creature made in God's image—lordship only over irrational creatures. "Hence, the first just men were established as shepherds of flocks, rather than as kings of men" (CG 19.15, p. 942). The order of social life in conditions of sin provides for mastery over the less rational (Augustine argues uncomfortably for social servitude as a punishment of sin), but the order of nature prescribes that the paterfamilias show "equal concern" for the welfare of "all the members" of his household (CG 19.16, p. 944).

The pilgrim's duty of care is thus properly the formal cause for the two social organizations which are bound together by relationships of command and obedience: the household and the city. The household and the city are different in kind—citizens are not members of a household; the city is not a household writ large—but they share the same formal (if not procedural) structure of command and obedience. The household is implicated in two ends, one penultimate and one ultimate. The household, Augustine says, "ought to be the beginning (*initium*), or little part, of the city; and every beginning has reference to some end proper to itself, and every part has reference to the integrity of the whole of which it is a part" (CG 19.16, p. 945). In the spirit of rule, the household is properly the formal cause of rule in the city. In the institutional form, the city is the penultimate end of the household. The household is the material, as it were, of the city—the constituent part. The rule of the household should aim to contribute to the earthly peace. But the pilgrim of faith also refers his duties of care to the heavenly peace as the ultimate end, and this heavenly city is no longer a form of association characterized by command and obedience.

In the exercise of duties of care, then, the pilgrim finds himself between penultimate and ultimate ends which are not wholly commensurate within the painting of history. Earthly and heavenly peace do overlap, but the latter opens more broadly. In extending his care from love of neighbor to love of household to love of city, the pilgrim finds himself in the position of the miserable judge who strives to balance competing and sometimes contradictory responsibilities.

The landscape of moral action is thus the field of the exercise of duty in structures of authority, rather than the field of the assertion of rights or power. And just as Cicero's *Republic* lurks behind the structure of Augustine's thought, so too does his work, *On Duties*. The teacher, Cicero says, teaches by knowledge; the city teaches by example (DT 1.1, p. 1). "For no part of life, neither public affairs nor private, neither in the forum nor at home, neither when acting on our own nor in dealings with another, can be free from duty. Everything that is honorable in a life depends upon its cultivation, and everything dishonorable upon its neglect" (DT 1.4, p. 3). Cicero too recognizes the challenge of navigating between and among conflicting duties and looks to both knowledge and example for instruction. He recognizes also the tension between the private affairs of the household and the public affairs of the forum. But his criterion is what is honorable, what is praiseworthy. Exemplarity here is both a moral and an aesthetic quality, what Plato would have called the fine—the beautiful and the good (*kalos kai agathos*). It is in the right cultivation of duty or responsibility that we become both beautiful and good.

The predicament of Augustine's pilgrim judge, then, is also the opportunity for refinement in what is beautiful and good. It is a creative tension, what Martin Luther King will later refer to as a "positive peace which is the presence of justice" as distinct from a "negative peace which is the absence of tension." Cicero ties duty honorably cultivated to virtue, which requires "instruction for a life that is shared" (DT 1.7, p. 4). For Cicero, the "impulse towards pre-eminence" derives from the desire for seeing the truth; one develops both greatness of spirit and disdain for human things when asked to obey that which is not just and lawful (DT 1.13, p. 7). That is, our nature recognizes both the power of words and deeds and their "order ... seemliness ... and limit." Only the human animal, says Cicero, "perceives the beauty, the loveliness, and the congruence of the parts, of the things that sight perceives. Nature and reason transfer this by analogy from the eyes to the mind, thinking that beauty, constancy, and order should be preserved, and much more so, in one's decisions and one's deeds" (DT 1.14, p. 8).

Like Augustine, Cicero's principle of justice pairs restraint with limited action. Our first duty is not to harm another; our second is to assist others as best we can, especially by being attentive, Cicero says, to common and private property (DT 1.20-22, pp. 9, 10). Nature puts three fields of duty upon us. The first is the duty to care for our own, and whatever property has fallen to us. But, Cicero says (citing Plato), "We are not born for ourselves alone." Our country and our friends also bind us in duty (DT 1.22, pp. 9, 10). Each sphere of duty has its respective ties that bind, but whatever the form of association, "nothing is more lovable and nothing more tightly binding than similarity in conduct that is good." The common bonds "created by kindnesses reciprocally given and received" hold people together "in an unshakeable fellowship" (DT 1.56, p. 23). The most durable ties are the moral bonds which emerge from the exercise of duty.

The honorable cultivation of duty takes up Cicero's theory on the classical virtues, but he emphasizes decorum, or seemliness, "what we might call the ordered beauty of a life, restraint and modesty, a calming of all the agitations of the spirit, and due measure in all things" (DT 1.94, p. 37). The ordered beauty of a moral life is akin to the physical beauty of a healthy body, but Cicero's description also sounds like what Augustine calls tranquility. This ordered beauty of a life shines out through a dual seemliness: a congruity with what is universal in human nature, viz., the right exercise of reason, and the measurement of our actions with respect to "the rule of our own nature"—that is, what is appropriate to and in keeping with our individual character, characteristics, and personality. It would be unseemly to "copy someone else's nature and ignore your own" (DT 1.107-110, pp. 42, 43).

Cicero's account of the dual nature of seemliness is paralleled by Augustine's own account of the created natural order. Cicero recognizes, with Augustine, the fundamental challenge: "Therefore all men should have this one object, that the benefit of each individual and the benefit of all together should be the same" (DT 3.26, p. 109). This alignment of individual and collective interest is only coherent in the language of duty—the instruction in life together requires learning by knowledge and example how to align one's private and public responsibilities. This, according to Cicero, is a law of nature.

The song of justice may only be composed and sung in the key of duty—the spirit of service to that which is beyond oneself, to those whom we are obliged to call our neighbors. The harmonization of voices is a restriction of freedom oriented toward the crescendo of justice beyond grievance. The pain of the past is not ignored or justified, but redeemed in its incorporation into the painting of a people, the depths of colors, the distress, that gives a community its richness, and renew the bonds of care in stronger sinews—if we have the moral eyes and ears to see the potential image, to hear the potential song.

4

Imagined Communities

Communities are symbolic entities, the product of imagination and of memory. Communities aim at some vision of the good; they are sustained by the practices which rise up and persist in the pursuit of that vision of the good. The imagination strives in the realm of intimations; memory builds upon the concrete. At the intersection of a community's imagination and memory, the cross-breeding as it were, are symbols—principles, events, places, narratives, people, actions—which define who a people are, who they have been, and what they are called to become. The symbols and community meld into one—indistinguishable because they are jointly expressions and objects of love. That is, a community as a symbolic entity takes on a kind of transcendence—it becomes something so loved that one might be willing to give it ultimate service, even death. This love of community plucks the mystic chords of our memory, and resonates in the chambers of our imagination in acts both of faith and of hope. In this, community is first and foremost a spiritual entity and only secondarily a material one. A community's prosperity is a material feature, but its vitality is essentially spiritual. A community whose vision of the good is colored primarily by prosperity will collapse in upon itself, absent an expansive spiritual vitality. A community so formed by transcendence is inexorably an expression of the triadic commandment of love of self, love of neighbor, and love of God, realized well or ill. That is, the worthiness or nobility of the transcendent orientation will form the worthiness or nobility of the community itself. As such, communities are constitutive of identity, requiring acts of both abandonment and possession.

Augustine's motif of the two cities is, then, fundamentally a recognition of the spiritual dimension of community. Communities are expressions not of matter, but of love. The two cities are multilayered symbolic manifestations not easily identified with physical instantiations in time or place. They are types, encapsulating the epic, lyric, and dramatic moments of an individual and social way of life. To say that a people is united by the common objects of their loves is to recognize the spiritual character of the community.

God has finished his works, according to Augustine, and yet his works have only just begun. God rests on the seventh day, and yet continues to create through the administration which succeeds the acts of creation. "God first created all things simultaneously at the beginning of the ages, creating some in their own substances and others in pre-existing causes" (LG 7.28.42, p. 31). So too, there is "a double activity of Providence, the natural and the voluntary"— God's hidden administration in the workings of nature and the voluntary "deeds of angels and men" (LG 8.9.17, p. 45; cf. 9.18.33, p. 93). The interplay of natural and voluntary Providence is still "ruled and governed" by God, because the extrinsic factors applied by human effort are nonetheless the work of creatures made by God (LG 8.8.16, p. 45).

"At this point," Augustine suggests, "the mind lifts up its gaze to consider the whole world like a great tree of creation." God creates; man "cultivates and guards." Even if man had not sinned, he still would have cultivated the land, voluntarily and not out of bodily need. "What more impressive and wonderful spectacle than this? Where is human reason better able to speak, as it were, to nature than when man sows the seed, plants a tree, transplants a bush, grafts a mallet-shoot, and thus asks (*interrogatur*), as it were, each root and seed what it can and cannot do," either intrinsically or when human effort is applied? (LG 8.8.15-16, pp. 44, 45). In cultivation, man both speaks to and questions nature in a conversation which yields growth in humans and the natural world alike. Creation brings us news of ourselves.

Voluntary Providence manifests itself in four aspects: learning, cultivating, governing, and the arts. "Of the voluntary working of Providence there are other signs: creatures are instructed and learn, fields are cultivated, societies are governed, the arts are practiced, and other activities go on both in the heavenly society and in this mortal society on earth; and the goods are provided for even with the help of the wicked, though all unwittingly." Human beings are the cultivators of the tree of creation of which they themselves are a very part. The natural whole is also a moral whole; human cultivation, whether of the natural world, the social-moral world, or the arts—the aesthetic world—is necessarily a form of self-cultivation. That is, we are to learn, and to help others (human and otherwise) learn the full potential of the possibilities of our natures.

In echoes of the catalog of peace, Augustine sketches the interplay of natural and voluntary Providence in body and soul. For the body, the natural cycle of birth, growth, and death is cultivated by the voluntary procurement of food, clothing, and the like. "So, too, in the case of the soul: by nature it is provided that it lives and has sensation; by voluntary action it is provided that it acquires knowledge and lives in harmony." Just as a gardener works extrinsically to assist a tree's internal development, so "medicine is an external help for the intrinsic natural forces" of the body. In the case of the soul, "instruction coming from an external source contributes to the interior happiness of nature." An "indifference to learning" on the part of the soul is like the neglect of healing for the body and the negligence in cultivating the tree (LG 8.9.17-18, p. 46). In the three-leveled analogy, it is clear that society is to be governed as a place of learning.

Full growth does not happen naturally; or rather, it is a part of the created order that the fullness of each creature is realized only through the interplay of both natural and voluntary activity. For non-human creatures, this means extrinsic assistance from God, even as our conversations with nature and society are part of our moral instruction. Indeed, Augustine speaks of cultivating as a kind of discipline (*disciplina*: teaching, instruction) which is natural to our creation and not a product of our fallen condition. Learning, cultivating, governing, and the practice of the arts are properly "a spiritual pleasure befitting of our dignity," and only become painful in our fallen condition (LG 8.10.20, p. 47; LG 8.9.18, p. 46).

To "cultivate and guard" carries a twofold movement. Cultivating is the spirit of inquiry and innovation, the exploration of the potential of measure, number, and weight. Guarding (*custodire*) entails a duty of care, a disposition to act in such a way as not to lose what one possesses. This is a conservative disposition, in the sense of conservation—conserving what we have; a duty to take care of what the past has bequeathed to us, as Cicero says. We cultivate by learning the rules or laws of nature by which potential is encoded and released. We guard by learning and obeying the rules or laws of God by which the beauty of the created order is enhanced and preserved. In our care, creation is made more fruitful; in God's care, we are made more just. "For just as man cultivates the earth not to make it earth but to develop it and make it fruitful, so God in a much deeper sense cultivates man, whom he has created and made man, so that he may be made just if he does not turn away from his Creator by pride" (LG 8.10.22-23, pp. 48, 49). Our work in the course of time is intended to be one of growth in learning in response to God's cultivation.

God's cultivation, of course, is intrinsic, in what we learn from nature, and extrinsic, in what we learn from each other. The physical and rational labor of cultivating nature imposes an internal, spiritual discipline. So too the process of governing a society imposes an internal spiritual discipline. Cultivating and guarding the social garden, as it were, is both a physical and a spiritual discipline. Plants and animals cannot disobey the laws of nature; they flourish according to the rules of their natures. Humans, as rational and spiritual creatures, are subject to the laws of nature; we flourish according to our free obedience to God. To cultivate and guard ourselves is "to be obedient under His rule rather than to live uncontrolled" and abuse our freedom. God placed man in Paradise, according to scripture,

> in order to cultivate him so that he would be just and guard him so that he would be safe, doing this by His rule, which is useful not for Him but for us. For God does not need our service, but we need His rule so that he may cultivate and guard us. Accordingly, He alone is the true Lord, because we serve Him not for His advantage and welfare but for ours. (LG 8.11.24, p. 50)

We are sinless in creation but not self-sufficient. Our obedience is not transactional but a form of self-care.

God's cultivation requires our voluntary participation through learning and obedience. "When God cultivates a just man," God's work is dissolved when man turns away. Just as air becomes luminous in the presence of light, "man is illuminated when God is present to him, but when God is absent, darkness is immediately upon him ... by a turning away of his will" (LG 8.12.26, p. 51). We come from dust, and to dust we shall return. But like dust in the air, we are luminous only insofar as we are in the light, that is, insofar as we cultivate and guard with God the justice of our own souls. "For we are His work of art not only in so far as we are human beings but also in so far as we are good" (LG 8.12.27, p. 51). We are good in our obedience to God and in exercising our duty to cultivate and guard the natural and the social order. In the fourfold movements of voluntary Providence, the intellectual and spiritual dimensions of learning and teaching and the practice of the arts frame or bracket the two fields of action: nature (reason) and society (will), where both are understood to be simultaneously natural and artificial—at once subject to intrinsic natural rules and the product of extrinsic voluntary cultivation and care.

For Augustine, the rule of bodily natures is naturally, intrinsically hierarchical. All creatures are subject to God; corporeal creatures subject to spiritual; the irrational to the rational; earthly to heavenly; female to male, the weak to the strong, the poor to the rich (LG 8.23.44, p. 64).[1] The rule of spiritual wills, however, is an overlay, as it were, of the scale of value. Here the hierarchy is moral, not physical. Hierarchies of a physical kind are erased or reformed by moral hierarchies—the rule of what is good supersedes physical inequality. God, says Augustine, submits himself to those who are good; the wicked are subjected to those who serve God: extrinsically (the realm of the body) through the command of the good, and intrinsically (the realm of the will) through the internal punishment which evil brings. Intrinsically, evil is its own punishment; extrinsically, wickedness is the true basis of social hierarchies.

Social life, then, is properly not the realization of natural physical inequality, but the transformation of physical inequalities by spiritual or moral hierarchy—the physical inequalities are a garden to be improved by spiritual cultivation. Created nature before the fall is still subject to improvement, with the aim that all creatures "may be not only healthy and productive but also fair to behold," though the perfection of created nature is found only in the life to come (LG 8.25.46, p. 65).

---

[1] Commentators, including Taylor (n. 104), are inclined to see Augustine as speaking of these hierarchies as the result of our fallen condition, not the created order. But Augustine is quite clear that this is the order of created nature, but also the occasion of improvement—this is a physical order, to be reformed according to the equality of the moral order.

Civil life, then, is a place of improving spiritual wills, a nourishment of the scale of value as a healing toward the beauty of physical hierarchy—the aim is that we become, spiritually, "fair to behold." Again, the field of physical nature is the field of material and efficient causality; the field of spiritual wills is that of formal and final causality. Rule, properly speaking, whether in the providential administration or in human social duties, is the realm of formal and final causality—physical force is properly subject to spiritual power.

What Augustine says about the society of angels is instructive. Intrinsically, angels are assisted by God's "eternity, truth, and love." Extrinsically, "they are helped only by the fact that they see one another and rejoice that they are joined in one society with God, that they see all creatures in these companions, and that therefore they give thanks and they praise their Creator" (LG 8.25.47, p. 66). They see the unity of fellowship and creation, and they give thanks. This expression of angelic society underscores, in a transposed context, the two moment of human social life: the symbolic and the liturgical, the signs of the city (*societas*) and the city's structures of worship (*latreia*).

When Augustine says that a people is united according to agreement about the common objects of their love, that love takes two directions—the symbols which form that love, and the expression of love in worship. The symbols form the worship and of course the worship shapes and gives rise to the symbols.

Signs, for Augustine, are stimuli of memory and imagination, the awakening of the divine in us. In his early dialogue, *On the Teacher*, Augustine tells us that signs are audible or visual cues which strike a chord of memory and bring to mind the signified (TC 1.2, p. 97). Signs may be internal, as when we pray silently, offering up "the 'sacrifice of justice' ... in the temple of the mind and in the bedchambers of the heart," not so that God may hear, "but that men ... by remembering might, with one accord, be raised to God" (TC 1.2, p. 96). Signs are more regularly external, and when we use signs to explicate other signs, the symbolic language becomes layered. But both the intrinsic and extrinsic use of signs presupposes a common apprehension of both the sign and the signified. That is, signs are inextricably social.

Nothing can be seen without signs; but the sign is not the signified. Signs are thus fraught with a dual ambiguity: we may misunderstand another's use of signs, and we may mistake the sign for the signified. For Augustine, the written word is a sign of the spoken word, which is a sign of the word heard within the mind, which is in turn a sign of the incorporeal signified understood without words at all. Therefore, the potential for mistaking the sign for the thing itself is considerable (TC 4.8, pp. 104ff).

Signs simultaneously, then, tend toward the visible (the social) and toward the invisible (the intelligible). Similarly, signs begin with visual or audible perceptions and move to memory, where physical perception and social convention recede to the intimate, solitary, ineffability of individual intellectual conception. We may agree on what the word "river" signifies, but each of us will have a different mental image of a river (TC 5.12, p. 110). Even the discussion of signs requires the use of signs, creating a self-reflexive, meta-analysis that Augustine describes playfully: "discussing words with words is as entangled as interlocking one's fingers and rubbing them together, where hardly anyone but the person doing it can distinguish the fingers that itch from the fingers scratching the itch" (TC 5.13-14, pp. 112, 113).

Despite the frequent convolution of signs, the knowledge of the thing is more valuable than the sign, though we often get waylaid by the ambiguity of the sign itself (TC 9.26-27, p. 129). The logic of signs, however, entails the logic of right ordering, of what is fitting and properly subordinate. The order of knowing is superior to the order of naming. In a nod to the skepticism of the Academics, Augustine cautions against letting disagreements about signs cause one to abandon the notion of truth altogether and so fall into a "great hatred and mistrust of reason" (TC 10.31, p. 134). Augustine's caution also reminds us of the trap of striving to agree on the literal meaning of names, as distinct from a shared understanding of meaning.

Augustine's argument in *On the Teacher* is reminiscent of that of Socrates in the *Meno*: knowledge is innate in the soul, but brought to light and clarified through the use of signs. The structure of speech, and of teaching, is thus in some sense upended. Augustine begins *On the Teacher* (dramatically a conversation with his 15-year-old son, Adeodatus), by saying that the purpose of words is to teach or remind; teaching collapses into reminding others of what they already know. As such, the putative authority of the teacher collapses into the authority of the word, which it turn folds into the internal authority of reason. "When I learned the thing itself, I trusted my eyes, not the words of another—though perhaps I trusted the words to direct my attention, that is, to find out what

I would see by looking ... words have force only to the extent that the remind us to look for things; they don't display them for us to know" (TC 11.36, p. 137).

Words, then, are not so much the tools of teaching but the conditions of learning. The social context of words and symbols participate not only in the illumination of knowledge, but in the formation of the soul. Augustine's discussion of signs is largely epistemological on the surface, but at every turn the dialogue points toward the moral. Indeed, the example of his conversation with Adeodatus is itself a sign of instruction, disclosing a form of dialogue and inquiry designed "to exercise the mind's strength and sharpness, with which we're able not only to withstand but also to love the heat and light of that region where the happy life is" (TC 8.21, p. 122). Dialogue itself is a sign which not only directs the participants' attention, but forms the attention, directs its desires, and refines its capacities. The form and quality of dialogue are not merely cognitive but spiritual and moral. Dialogue is the condition under which our loves are formed.

At the heart of the content and form of Augustine's dialogue are questions, the catalyst of inquiry and discovery. The quality of dialogue would seem to depend upon the capacity of words and symbols to generate questions. "How do you suppose we learn, after all, if not when we ask questions?" (TC 1.1, p. 94). This is Adeodatus's second utterance and first question at the beginning of the dialogue, in answer to Augustine's query, "When we speak, what does it seem to you we want to accomplish?" Reasoned speech is distinctive to human beings, but for what purpose? Teaching, learning, reminding; the three are inseparable. Questions are those uses of speech which prompt learning through the exterior stimulus of an internal memory. Prayer is the external and internal reminder for others and ourselves of our duty to God. Augustine addresses singing on several occasions, though he tries in passing to distance it from speech proper. But the kernel of Augustine's framework might be summarized as such: we speak (i.e., we exercise our distinctive human quality) to stimulate the memory and imagination (largely through questions) to recognize or awaken the soul's latent knowledge of created nature (including oneself) and God, and to engage in the pleasure of singing, especially songs of praise to God. Signs prompt us to learn, to know, and to praise.

The culmination of learning and knowing in praise puts epistemology in a doxological and therefore moral framework.

We only worship what is worthy of praise, and so to recognize the noble and dismiss the ignoble is a fundamental dimension of knowing—knowing facts entails also judging value or meaning.

Augustine's dialogue *On the Teacher* is ripe with clues in the form of the texts he uses as examples in his conversation with Adeodatus. The first, recognizing that articulated sound appeals to "the hidden parts of the rational soul," is 1 Corinthians 3:16: "Do you not know that you are the temple of God and that the Spirit of God dwells within you?" And immediately thereafter, Psalm 4:4-5: "Speak in your hearts and be stricken in your bedchambers; offer up the sacrifice of justice, and hope in the Lord." Shortly thereafter, Augustine introduces the first classical text, from Vergil's Aeneid: "If nothing from so great a city it pleases the gods be left ..."—Aeneas's words to his father, Anchises, on the pending destruction of Troy (TC 1.2-2.3, pp. 96, 97). This juxtaposition of Paul and the Psalms with Vergil, which frames the dialogue, juxtaposes the presence of God in the temple of the individual soul with the departure of the gods from the city.

Augustine's next quotation is from Terrence: "Good words, if you please!"—a slave's ironic response to his abusive master (TC 4.9, p. 106). Augustine later takes up the question, what do we signify when we speak the syllables ho-mo (*homo*, man)? *utrum homo homo sit?*—whether man is man, or perhaps "whether 'man' is man." What is a human being? What is the nature of the human being? What is the meaning, in the deepest sense, of the word, *homo*? (TC 8.23, p. 124)

All of these examples are deployed specifically to illustrate parts of speech, and the linguistic-philosophical analysis rightly occupies the reader's full attention. But the simultaneously deeper meaning, inseparable from the grammatical, is an ongoing moral teaching illustrated through textual samples. What space does God (or the gods) occupy or abandon?—a question both existential and political. Troy here echoes Augustine's later attempt, in the *City of God*, to account for the gods' abandonment of Rome in the sack of 410. Where do the gods abide?, similarly, is inseparable from inquiring about what the human being is and means. And so the next quotation, from Persius's *Satires*, is: "But this man is besotted with vice ...," (TC 9.28, p. 130) echoing the abusive relationship of master and slave, which in Augustine's dialogue leads to a discussion of how we signify and teach virtue (or its absence). How do we know what we are looking for, such that we recognize it when it presents itself to us? Augustine quotes next Isaiah: "Unless you believe, you shall not understand" (TC 11.37, p. 138). This leads Augustine to his conclusion that Christ is the inner teacher, that the indwelling of God in the temple of the soul or in the temples of the city depends upon human beings who are engaged in overcoming vice through a knowledge of virtue. This knowledge is itself dependent upon the activity of faith seeking understanding, where faith itself is understood to be a rational act, an obedience to the laws of reason, the deployment of intellect amid an honest assessment of what is known and what is unknown through the science of signs.

This excursus brings us back to the symbolic character of social life as a feature of both memory and imagination. What do we signify when we speak the word "city"? What is the meaning of "community" or "society"? How are we to pursue this inquiry with the knowledge that our words themselves are reflexively shaped by the social-linguistic conceptions of the good, of justice, of power, etc.? In a world of "bad words," how do we discover the "good words, please"?

Let us consider the signs Augustine has presented: the human being, the household, the city, and the church. Each prompts a mental image, a distinct imagined community. These imagined communities are formed by the memory of the communities that I have already experienced, and the comparison of those communities against that inner, un-signified knowledge of what the community should be. My image of the city is shaped by the city that I know, but is qualified by the imagination of the city which ought to be, imagined in relation to my memory of a perfect city. My experience of justice is measured by my inner conception of justice as I have discovered implanted in me. Of course, our attempts to think about justice are clouded by the intrusion of corporeal images. When we engage in dialogue about justice with others, it is necessary for us, then, "to paint, as it were, a picture of justice and wisdom in their minds with shapes and colors, for they cannot think of them as incorporeal." But, Augustine continues, when we are "moved by justice or wisdom to praise these virtues or do some deed in accordance with them," then of course we move beyond corporeal images to the incorporeal reality (LG 10.24.40, p. 128). The visual symbol becomes an invisible exemplarity which yields praise and action. The structure of the exemplarity: cognition-thought, praise, action.

The visual symbol teaches, it forms desires, it calls out for praise and imitation, but only properly insofar as it approximates what is good and beautiful and true. The symbol of imagined community is therefore not only complex, but complicated and not transparent, and while worthy of our love, the imagined community is not worthy of our unqualified love. This is reserved for that final, beatific vision which renders the virtues effortless and resolves them into love itself.

The one virtue and the whole of virtue there is to love what you see, and the supreme happiness is to possess what you love. For there beatitude is imbibed at its source, whence some few drops are sprinkled upon this life of ours, that amid the trials of this world we may spend our days with temperance, fortitude, justice, and prudence. It is surely in pursuit of this end, where there will be secure peace and the unutterable vision of truth, that man undertakes the labor of restraining his desires, of bearing adversities, of relieving the poor, of opposing deceivers. (LG 12.26.54, p. 217)

The object of love thus oscillates between what it sees and what it longs to see, where what is longed for may be undiscovered or intimated, and if discovered still not fully known. In this sense, love is both an abandonment and a possession—a grasping hold of some imperfect recollection and an abandonment toward an imagined good which is not yet fully realized. This love, for Augustine, has two orientations: it folds in on itself in inordinate self-love, or it expands outward by placing ordinate self-love in the order of created nature which cultivates the love of God and neighbor.

The inordinate attachment of the heart to one's own good leads to a privation of one's true good. Augustine uses the word *privatus* as a synonym for *proprius*—what is one's own can become private rather than bound to creation, and so the private marks a privation, a withdrawal. Private interest is the opposite of justice and comes from the spirit of pride; "privacy" is a loss—we do not gain when we deprive ourselves or things of their rootedness in the common good. It is this contrast between the private and the common (what is attached to the whole)—not understood in terms of property ownership but as the property, propriety or quality, of one's loves—

that frames Augustine's first full articulation of the two cities as an orienting motif:

> There are, then, two loves, of which one is holy, the other unclean; one turned towards the neighbor, the other centered on self; one looking to the common good, keeping in view the society of saints in heaven, the other bringing the common good under its own power, arrogantly looking to domination; one subject to God, the other rivaling Him; one tranquil, the other tempestuous; one peaceful, the other seditious; one preferring truth to false praise, the other eager for praise of any sort; one friendly, the other envious; one wishing for its neighbor what it wishes for itself, the other seeking to subject its neighbor to itself; one looking for its neighbor's advantage in ruling its neighbor, the other looking for its own advantage. These two loves started among the angels, one love in the good angels, the other in the bad; and they have marked the limits of the two cities established among men under the sublime and wonderful providence of God, who administers and orders all that He creates; and one city is the city of the just, and the other city is the city of the wicked. With these two cities intermingled to a certain extent in time, the world [*saeculum*] moves on until they will be separated at the last judgment. (LG 11.15.20, pp. 147, 148)[2]

If we think of these cities as actual institutions, we deflate, as it were, the fullness of the symbols as exemplary types. The two cities are orienting, exemplary images of social life which disclose the loves that animate them. As with conventional citizenship, the citizenship of the two cities, respectively, entails loyalty, identity, solidarity, and responsibility (in the sense of a bond of action): justice and the common good, or wickedness and the private good. The images reflect aspirations—they are expressions of love—and form those aspirations—they reinforce the love expressed. In addition to being descriptive, they are normative—toward good and evil—they are measures which articulate competing scales of value: justice (rendering to each what is due as members of the created order) and pride (viewing all as due primarily to oneself).

---

[2]Note that this passage is from *On the Literal Meaning of Genesis*. Augustine goes on to say that perhaps he will write a book on the two cities, God willing.

These, then, are the limit conditions of social life, in which human experience at all levels of the catalog of peace tends more or less toward the tranquility of order. These two emblems of fundamental love are "intermingled to a certain extent in time"—they are distinguishable but inseparable, both socially and within each soul. And, together, they are the crucible in which we learn to be our more divine selves. Our journey in time, as pilgrims or exiles, takes place in the double helix, as it were, of the two cities.

The emblems of the two cities teach by exemplarity, and exemplarity is expressed definitively through law. The law is, as it were, the word of the city, pointing to the encounter with social life that lies behind the sign. Law functions not only at the epistemological level—it is a dictate of reason—but also on the moral level, as a command: it teaches and enjoins, it binds to action. Just as words direct our attention from the corporeal to the incorporeal, so too laws train our souls to attend to divine things, to obey the laws of creation and the creator. Law forms through external command the desire to obey an internal command.

It is tempting to read the two cities as gnostic competitors, and that is often how the motif is understood. And for good reason: the binary formulation is stark, the damnation of one and the celebration of the other is clear. But this is true of the citizenship, the disposition of the soul, and not, as it is often presented and usually understood, the reduction of the motif to the institutions of church and state. Actual social life is animated by the imagined citizenship of the two cities: actual cities are formed and inhabited by citizens who feel the tug of each city within them, who strive for the public rather than the private, and vice versa. And actual churches contain, as Augustine says, both the wheat and the tares.

In formulating the two cities, Augustine wishes to emphasize the two ways of being in social life—living as a pilgrim and as an exile. But we are all both, at the same time, pilgrims and exiles in the journey of this life. And the cities, imagined and actual, are inextricably linked as the conditions of our education. Augustine wishes us to understand both the contrast of the two cities, and the dynamic tension they produce, as in a fugue, or the two poles of an ellipse. There are independent lines, distinct and dissonant; two foci with elliptical pulls. Within these fields we walk as pilgrims and exiles to varying degrees—sometimes leaning toward one pole, sometimes the other; sometimes crossing from one contrapuntal line to another—learning (or not learning) to find our way to the rest that is the proper realization of our place in the scale of value. That is, we struggle to become pilgrims who find our way home.

Under the aspect of our created nature, the city is the order of intellect regulated by positive law. Its object, properly, is the regulation of the physical, of the body—the ordering of material things, of what is mine and thine. Under the aspect of our fallen condition, the city must be content with ignorance. The law teaches in two moments: in the pedagogical moment (the laws instruct) and in the penal moment (the laws constrain and punish). What we do not learn from the pedagogy of the law, we may come to learn from material punishment. Just as, ideally, we learn moderation from the pain of a hangover, so too we learn social moderation when our undue attachment to self and material things is chastened by fines or imprisonment. By itself, this form of social life can instruct and correct, but it cannot heal.

In created nature, the church—our shorthand for spiritual community—is the order of will regulated by moral law. Whereas the city asks us to do the good, the church enjoins us also to will the good. Where positive law has as its object the outward, physical action—to respect what is mine and thine—the church is the place devoted to helping us learn to regulate the internal, spiritual motion of our hearts—what is mine and God's. In our fallen condition, the church must contend with the infirmity of our wills—our capacity to know the good, and even to do the good, without wholeheartedly willing it. In this spiritual form of social life, we have the prospect of healing.

The two spheres of teaching and learning overlap, are intertwined. In the process of learning from the law (whether good or bad) we become habituated to doing the good, and possibly to willing the good, and as the infirmities of our hearts are healed the law becomes written upon our hearts. The more these two environments tend toward virtue, the more conducive they are to the fullness of learning to which the pilgrim is called. But Augustine is clear that bad laws and corrupted communities also teach by a negative example which, in some sense, is still just. In cities and in churches alike, ancient ways and institutions and exemplary leaders are the only safeguards. When Augustine says that a people gets the rulers it deserves, his sense is that there is a natural tendency or law of inertia in social life—a people whose social organization permits tyranny must learn, through hardship, how to form a polity of freedom and virtue. A people whose church becomes corrupt has neglected its spiritual foundation and formation. In this, justice and injustice are both relative conditions of dignity and schools of virtue which both shape and reflect the conditions of our learning. One constrains the exile; the other forms the pilgrim.

The constraint of the exile has as its object one's relation to one's neighbor in material social life. Here, *lex* aims for the realization of *ius* understood as material property—the reconciliation of divergent wills with respect to what is mine and yours. In this register the city strives to bring *lex* and *ius* into alignment given a particular people at a particular time in a particular place under particular circumstances. The alignment of *lex* and *ius* operates at the level of *scientia*: positive law operates with temporal knowledge, giving rise to civil virtues which are "truth-like" in their approximation of the divine knowledge (*sapientia*) (AA, 3.17.37, pp. 87, 88). "The law of the people deals with acts it must punish in order to keep peace among ignorant men, insofar as deeds can be governed by men" (FW 1.5.40, p. 12). Law aligning with *ius* creates a space of order in which learning can occur according to the principle of justice: first do no harm; second do good as far as possible. The weight of *lex-ius* is on the former, the purview of the city.

The formation of the pilgrim shifts the register of *lex* from *ius* to *caritas*, having as its object the properties of one's own and one's neighbor's spiritual life. Here, *lex* aims for the realization of love understood as propriety—the reconciliation of what is ours in relation to God. *Lex-caritas* is not bound by place or time— the form of the expression of love may vary, but the essence of love is the working out of the order of nature, not the contingent character of time and place. *Lex-caritas* seeks what is proper to each according to created nature, and so operates on the level of wisdom (*sapientia*) not knowledge (*scientia*).

The intertwining of city and church, distinct but circling around each other as in a dance, or as musical counterpoints to one another, is thus the recognition of two distinct but complementary spheres: matter and spirit, body and soul, and so two distinct but complementary formulations of law—*lex-ius* and *lex-caritas*. The former provides a framework of temporal peace; the latter forms the soul to a heavenly peace. Each gives to the other what is due. In the order of social life we owe each other peace; in the order of spiritual life we owe each other good according to the scale of created nature.

So, when Augustine writes that "the law of liberty is the law of love" (*Letter* 167.6.4), he refers to the expression of *ius* understood as obedience to both the principle of eternal reason and of divine love.

Nestled, as it were, between the two imagined communities of city and church are three micro-social communities: the household, friendship, and marriage. Whereas city and church are distinct but intertwined, household, friendship, and marriage are mixed in the sense that each demands both *ius* and *caritas*, and in each the material and spiritual are joint objects of teaching and learning. In civic life, action pertains to those who are more distant in natural or social bond; households, friendship and marriage carry responsibilities that are more directly "one's own." In the household, friendship, and marriage, the civic virtues and spiritual virtues combine to adduce the goods of the body and soul simultaneously. In civic life, "do no harm" is the principal injunction. In the household, friendship, and marriage, Augustine adds, with great weight, "do good as far as possible," where "good" is understood to include the fullness of one's spiritual life. Here *lex-ius* gives way to *lex-caritas*; persons are not ruled but served; there is mutual support in the suppression of vices.

Neither the household nor friendship is a sign, the way the two cities are. But each reflects an escalating sphere of responsibility: the household is oriented toward the virtues of utility under the rule of the *paterfamilias*; friendship toward moral virtue in equality, except for friendship with God, which is a relationship of radical inequality (more precisely, incommensurability, since equality presumes a likeness in kind). Marriage is a special sign as a consequence of its status as a sacrament. Marriage is a sign of the union of Christ and his Church. Household and friendship are spiritual but not sacramental; they are nature, whereas two becoming one is supernatural.

Communion in differentiation, or differentiation leading to domination. These are the motions of the signification of the two cities. Spiritual life and social life properly aim toward the progressive alignment of the individual private good and the public good. Marriage is that unique sacramental sign which discloses the full possibility of graced communion: two souls made one flesh, echoing the sacramental communion of the church, reflecting the Word made flesh, the full union of the human and the divine. *Lex-*

ius is resolved in *lex-caritas*. The imagined communities foster obedience to the law of liberty which is the law of love.

Our analysis this far has remained at the level of created nature, compromised by our fallen condition. We have explored the contours of social life—in civic and in spiritual registers—apart from grace, for Augustine's own logic does so. But the opportunities to learn to love are completed only by the full communion of creator and created. That is, the path from "our original justice" as Augustine calls it, to our perfected justice entails not the elevation of the wholeness of creation apart from God, but the elevation of the wholeness of creation in God. This natural path requires a supernatural act, conceived as both formal and efficient cause. Christ Incarnate is both an emblem and a bridge—a self-emptying manifestation of power in *forma servi*, in the form of service. In Christ, the disposition of power in service to the good of others rather than self becomes supernaturally manifest to a degree and in a kind which created nature cannot effect.

Augustine's motif of the two cities in *The City of God* is the culmination of a complex set of ideas. We have seen its preliminary formulation in *On the Literal Interpretation of Genesis*, but two early dialogues help us view the double helix of the two imagined communities with greater nuance. In *On the Teacher*, Augustine is concerned with how, through language, we come to know what is good. In *On the Free Choice of the Will*, he explores how the will comes to judge what is higher and lower. Both dialogues emphasize the concentration of attention to what is true and to what is good, and in so doing to our both becoming and contributing to what is beautiful.

If *On the Teacher* is an extended dialogical meditation on how we learn, *On the Free Choice of the Will* is an extended reflection on whether we learn to sin. More precisely, Evodius, Augustine's interlocutor, asks, "from whom ... have we learned how to sin?" (FW 1.1.4, p. 3) The premise of the question is that sin is not natural or innate, but learned; as posed, the question is not metaphysical or ontological, but epistemological and moral. Evil, Augustine replies, is not learned—evil is a privation of learning, a lack of *disciplina*. "To do evil is to turn from education" (FW 1.1.6, p. 4). If education is a good, then it cannot be the source of evil, and therefore no true teacher can be a teacher of evil (FW 1.1.9, p. 5). Evil is a failure of understanding. And, as Augustine concludes in *On the Teacher*, if Christ is ultimately the inner magister—that is, if all learning has its source in the divine, evil cannot be learned. Evil is an interruption of our journey in learning.

Augustine is clear that his focus is not on intelligence as such—evil is not an intellectual incapacity, but a consequence of ignorance, of the overcoming of the desire for truth by the desire to dominate, and by fear. Evil is a turning away of one's love from eternal truth and the triumph of "the love of those things which a man can lose against his will" (FW 1.4.30-1, p. 10). Augustine here expresses what Aristotle calls "self-sufficiency," not autonomy or isolation but a radical dependence on what is rightly transcendent rather than temporal. To will according to the scale of natural value insulates one against the suffering that inevitably comes, through force, accident, or intrinsic dissatisfaction, from loving inordinately what comes to be and passes away. But even this realization is painful, as Augustine demonstrates when reflecting on the death of his friend in *Confessions* Book 4. It was not evil to have loved his friend dearly, but in loving his friend inordinately as an eternal rather than a temporal good, Augustine learns, through suffering, to recalibrate his desires.

This kind of learning is of course not the purview of temporal law, though eternal and natural law may impress upon us an understanding of life which might be "ordered in the highest degree" (FW 1.6.50-1, pp. 14,15). That is, we are most ordered when the emotions and desires are mastered by the mind or spirit aligning themselves with the eternal law and so coming to will the virtues (FW 1.13.89-98, pp. 25–28). Resistance to a just temporal law is a sign of an inordinate love of temporal things. Those who abide by the eternal law do not fear or need the temporal law, which properly concerns itself only with temporal things. In this sense, temporal law is the law proper to pilgrims: "temporal law commands ... that men should possess these things which may be called ours for a time (when men cling to them out of desire) by that right (*ius*) by which peace and human society are preserved—insofar as they can be preserved amid these circumstances" (FW 1.15.107-11, pp. 30, 31).

Here the motif of the two cities is nascently expressed as two kinds of men loving two kinds of things, temporal and eternal. And while temporal things by their nature are uncertain and subject to change, they nonetheless have "their own order and complete the universe through their own particular beauty" (FW 1.16.114-118, pp. 33, 34). This is the note on which Augustine concludes *On the Free Choice of the Will* Book 1, the arc of which begins with our privation of learning and ends with learning how to order our desires and temporal things in such a way that the love of the law makes good things beautiful.

Book 2 of *On the Free Choice of the Will* pursues the insight that justice necessarily raises questions of transcendence. I have a sense of what is right for me and right for you, but how can I be certain that I am right about either? As with *On the Teacher*, Augustine recognizes that he cannot teach his interlocutor, only help him find the answer himself in accordance with his inner teacher (FW 2.2.9, p. 37).

The investigation of transcendence requires both belief and understanding. Belief is not merely a propositional affirmation, but a disposition of the whole soul become fit to understand (FW 2.2.15-19, pp. 38, 39). What we know we know by referring sense data to reason, which in turn is self-reflexive. Reason comprehends itself by itself. The "inner sense" is also confirmed or rejected by reason as part of reason's iterative journey, "now struggling to arrive at truth, now ceasing to struggle, sometimes reaching it and sometimes not" (FW 2.5.50-52, p. 42). This journey is individual and social, for while we each have different senses, experiences, and judgments, reason is in principle common to all. In an epistemological parallel to private right and public law, we are challenged to align those things which we consume or perceive only according to our own individual nature with those things which are common or public which can be perceived by all without being appropriated, changed, or destroyed (FW 2.7.59, p. 50). Augustine is here echoing Heraclitus: "Although the logos is common, the many live as if they had a wisdom of their own" (Heraclitus, 1. P. 77 Fr. 2).

While reason is shared, Augustine observes, there are rival claims to wisdom. Wisdom is the source of virtue, for living justly requires an understanding of relative value—of what is more worthy than something else, what things are equal, and what things are appropriate to what place. That is, wisdom furnishes judgments about relative and absolute value, understood epistemologically, morally, and aesthetically (FW 2.10.110-117, pp. 60–62). Of course, the highest things defy adequate expression in words, and so exhausted are we by the challenge of articulating the ineffable, we are prone to relax into the ease of talking about lower, more familiar things. Nonetheless, wisdom, like a fire, warms the things that lie near it, Augustine says. Wisdom is both light and heat, and truth is both the source of our freedom and a common possession the enjoyment of which is limited only by our attention. In what is arguably the structural and rhetorical climax of *On the Free Choice of the Will* Book 2, and thus of the work itself (comprising 3 books in all), Augustine describes a kind of rapture:

> When the will to enjoy is continually present, the beauty of truth and wisdom does not shut out those who have come to hear because of the large crowd; it does not pass with time, and does not move in space. It is not cut short by night or shadows. It does not depend on the sense of the body. It is near to all men who have chosen it and love it. It is eternal for all. It is in no one place, yet it is never away. Without, it advises; within, it teaches. It changes for the better all who behold it, and is not changed for the worse by anyone. No man passes judgment on truth, and no man judges well without it. For this reason it is clear that the beauty of truth and wisdom is, without doubt, superior to our minds, which become wise only through this beauty and which make judgments, not about it but through it, on other things. (FW 2.14.147-152, p. 70)

Wisdom calls us back to that which truly delights by means of the form imprinted upon our souls at creation. "Your beckoning is all the beauty of creation. By the very beauty of his work the artist somehow beckons the spectator, instead of fixing his eyes wholly on the beauty of the work he has made, to pass over this beauty and to look in fondness at him who made it" (FW 2.16.168, p. 74). The beckoning of wisdom properly prompts praise, and since "nothing can give itself form," the journey toward wisdom both satisfies and strengthens the desire to complete the journey, heaping beauty upon beauty (FW 2.17.172, p. 76). The departure from this beauty, this form, is a failure of attention; sin is "a defective movement (*defectivus motus*)," what he will later call the *causa deficiens*.

Book 1 ends with the calling to make the good things of creation beautiful. Book 2 concludes with the recognition of our failure to do so as a result of a defective movement, a relaxation of attention. Book 3, then, takes up the means by which our attention to divine beauty is restored. In ruling ourselves unjustly, Augustine says, we are justly unhappy. In turn, our unhappiness is proportional to our lack of form, our distance from the warmth of wisdom, our disordered embrace of the transient at the expense of what is permanent. In stepping out of the order of nature which properly belongs to us, we cease to beautify creation, even though the capacity to sin is part of nature's beauty (FW 3.6.66-3.9.99, pp. 101-109).

> God made all natures, not only those which will continue in virtue and justice, but also those which will sin. He did not make them so that they might sin, but so that they might adorn the universe whether they will to sin or whether they do not so will. If the universe did not have souls which could attain the very peak of the order in the whole creation—such that, if they chose to sin, the universe would be weakened and would totter—something great would be missing in creation; indeed, the universe would lack a thing so important that once it was removed, the stability and harmony of the creation would be disturbed. (FW 3.11.113, p. 113)

The freedom of the will completes the panoply of possibility in creation. The will's failure in sin detracts from creation's beauty, but the power to recover the will's proper happiness makes created nature even more beautiful. A sinful creature restored "reaches his highest place through the humility of repentance" (FW 3.5.55, p. 98).

The journey to repentance and restoration is both natural and supernatural. Both natural law and positive law place things in their right order, and punishment by law "forces them [i.e., disordered natures] to comply with the beauty of the universe" (FW 3.9.95, p. 108). The soul's natural judgment "prefers wisdom to error and peace to difficulty" even before the habits of virtue are etched in the soul. Ignorance and difficulty spur us on to the journey of learning which leads ultimately to the encounter with the inner teacher, who in turn teaches that we are in need of divine assistance (FW 3.20.190-191, p. 131). Faith is God's gift of assistance, supported by mercy, as we learn to recover the unity to which we were created. As rational beings, we resist ambiguity and, in our desire for knowledge, impose a unity on experience. By faith we begin to bring our own framework of unity into alignment with the natural created order (FW 3.23.238, p. 142).

So it is that we are suspended between the folly of our own knowledge and the divine wisdom. Our predicament, Augustine says, is that we have the ability to understand a command which we ought to obey, even if in ignorance and weakness we do not obey it (FW 3.24.242-244, p. 143). The two imagined cities are not enough. The peace which derives from the just arrangement of temporal goods is not sufficient to draw us to obedience to the command we know we ought to obey, nor is the spiritual community's sense of transcendence sufficient. Natural and social punishment is an unavoidable stimulus to learn under the promise of redemption, but a further sign and sacrament is needed. Augustine concludes *On the Free Choice of the Will* with God's presentation of Christ "for the imitation of his humility." The Cross has a fundamentally pedagogical value, teaching us loving humility through sacrifice and service, and calling us to contemplate higher rather than lower things, to delight in "the beauty of justice" and so to bathe in the Sabbath rest.

5

The Arc of Justice and the Arrow of Beauty

The imitation of humility leads to the beauty of justice, but where is the beauty in suffering? In crucifixion, Christ transforms the greatest injustice into the greatest justice. Sinless in body and spirit, the Incarnate Christ is subject to social punishment (of the body) and to spiritual agony (not the agony of sin as subject to the laws of nature, but the agony of experience and the human sense of forsakenness). In the very ugliness of the crucifixion, divine beauty shines through.

Augustine's *On the Trinity* is rightly seen as a doctrinal treatise on the triune God. That said, its propositional content pales beside enactment of the discipline of the soul's gaze to contemplate the divine wholeness. Augustine's aim is not to tell, but to show; to lead the mind to a contemplation which is beyond reason—not irrational, but not overly rational. He begins *On the Trinity* by cautioning against the sophistries of those who allow themselves to be deceived "through an unreasonable and misguided love of reason," a reason which does not obey its own limits (TR 1.1.1, p. 65). Augustine seeks to train the mind of his reader to know the Creator, to prepare the attention for an encounter with the divine in all fullness. The poetic coda which constitutes the fifteenth and final book of *On the Trinity* notes that the first fourteen books dealt discursively with things that are difficult to apprehend all at once. Like the narrative account of creation, discursive reasoning is a prelude, a preparation for apprehending things in a single instant (TR 15.1.4, p. 397). The more closely we look at the working of the mind, the "more our language begins to stagger, and our attention fails to persevere until our understanding if not our tongue can arrive at some clear result" (TR 15.2.13, p. 405). The tongue may stop short, but the understanding carries on in wordless clarity.

About what things can we have clarity of understanding if not clarity of speech? As in *On the Teacher*, in *On the Trinity* speech recedes in the wordless silence of understanding. To be sure, Augustine strives to understand the unity of the Godhead—Father, Son, and Holy Spirit—in reference to the unity of the human person—memory, intellect, and will. But scholarly considerations of Trinitarian doctrine and theological anthropology have obscured the *basso continuo* of the work—the pulsing rhythm of justice.

Reading *On the Trinity* as an exploration of the arc of justice casts Christ's Incarnation and suffering in a different light. Justice as righteousness or holiness is recast as justice as wholeness. The "justice of faith" (Rom. 4:13) nurses the mind back to full vigor, strengthening and purifying its sight so as to be able to gaze upon the dazzling light of supreme goodness (TR 1.1.3-4, pp. 66, 67). In purifying mind and heart, the justice of faith yields the justice of service or worship: *douleuein*, serving one another in charity; *latreuein*, the service owed to God (TR 1.2.13, p. 73). The object of faith, and the union of the two forms of worship, is the Incarnate Word who, as Mediator, restores us to health. Taking the *forma servi* in a way that did not lose the *forma dei*, Christ both descends to us and raises us to a status of equality. The Son is equal to the Father by nature, but is inferior by condition. We are unequal to God by nature, but can be raised to a kind of equality by condition. "In the form of God he made man, in the form of a servant he was made man" (TR 1.3.14, p. 74).

From the beginning, then, Augustine is looking for ways to understand and describe equality and differentiation—equality of nature, inequality or differentiation of form. The *forma dei* and the *forma servi* are the "two resonances" to which the scriptures are tuned, and to which our understanding of the Son must also be tuned (TR 1.4.22, p. 82). The weight of *On the Trinity*, then, leans upon understanding the justice of the form, not of the nature. The logical puzzle of the Trinitarian relations (or the internal human workings of memory, intellect, and will) is also the logical puzzle of holding the unity of equality and differentiation, equality and hierarchy.

The Incarnation and crucifixion of Christ are thus symbolic of this unity of equality and hierarchy—divine lordship and human service. The irruption of Christ in time is a visible historical symbol, but in his ascension, he is equally significant: "it was necessary for the form of the servant to be removed from their sight" lest the Word made flesh become an object of idolatry rather than an icon pointing to the Father. In response to this caution, Augustine too tries to write in such a way as to point not to the word but the God behind the word, the Word behind the word. He seeks to develop in himself and the reader an intellectual and spiritual discipline of seeing the same person in different forms (TR 1.4.25-27, pp. 84–86).

Books 1 and 15 are the bookends, as it were, of the establishment and transcendence of form. The justice of faith leads to the justice of worship which leads to the *forma servi*, which in turn points to the *forma dei*, the form beyond all forms. At the structural and philosophical center of the work, Book 8, is Augustine's extended meditation on justice.

Structurally, Book 8 is the peak of the parabolic organization of *On the Trinity*, what Edmund Hill calls the "change over to inward mode; link between God and *mens*," i.e., the pivot point from the discussion of the visible theophanies of the divine missions (Books 2–4) and the linguistic logical analysis of the Trinity (Books 5–7) to the psychological analogies of the Trinity (Books 9–11), culminating in the articulation of the human image (Books 12–14) (TR p. 27; Hill's introduction). Just as, in *On the Teacher*, Augustine poses the question, "what is homo?," here in *On the Trinity* Book 8 he asks, what do we love in a good man? The answer: we love his just mind.

The philosophical problem Augustine is trying to solve is this: how can we love that which we do not know? We love a man's just mind even if we do not know what justice is. For we know the body or mind of another because we have some experience of our own body and mind. Justice is "a sort of beauty of mind," and if we recognize it in another, it is because we have some intimation of it within ourselves, from an inner source. I know justice even if I only experience its fragments. That mind is just which "knowingly and deliberately, in life and conduct, gives each man what is his own." This memory of justice is unlike the mental image I have of Carthage, Augustine says, or my imagination of what Alexandria might be like. When I know a just mind, "I am perceiving something that is present to me, and is present to me even if I am not what I perceive." It is "wonderfully surprising" for a mind to see a just mind while itself not being the just mind that it sees. Minds becomes just "by cleaving to that same form which they behold, in order to be formed by it and become just minds." It is not enough to perceive a just mind, but by actually "living justly" and owing "no man anything but to love one another" (Rom. 13:8) we become formed to justice (TR 8.4.9, pp. 248–51). Augustine has reformulated the classic definition of justice in terms of love. We love ourselves and our neighbor either because they are just or in order for ourselves and our neighbor to become more just.

Again, love of neighbor and love of self resolve themselves into the love of God, since when one does what God commands one loves God. When a man loves his neighbor, "it follows that above all he loves love itself," for God is love and love is God. "There you are, God is love. Why should we go running round the heights of the heavens and depths of the earth looking for him who is with us if only we should wish to be with him?" (TR 8.5.11, pp. 252, 253) Love of neighbor perfected becomes love of brother, "the perfection of justice"—a love which recognizes a fellow citizen as a biological relation. "When therefore we love our brother out of love, we love our brother out of God" and come to see both neighbor and God with the inner, spiritual vision of love (TR 8.5.12, pp. 253, 254).

The man of whose just mind Augustine speaks is St. Paul, who is both exemplary in his justice and a catalyst which stirs us to embrace the form on which his life was formed. So, we are pointed to Christ, for it is in God "that we observe that unchanging form of justice which we judge that a man should live up to." While Paul is an exemplary approximation of justice, Christ as *forma servi* was uniquely "harmoniously adjusted to this form" (*huic formae coaptatem et congruentem fuisse*). Christ as *forma servi* is the manifestation in time of the form of justice (TR 8.5.13, pp. 254, 255).

God is love and justice. Christ, as *forma servi*, "justices," as with G. M. Hopkins:

> I say móre: the just man justices;
> Keeps grace: thát keeps all his goings graces;
> Acts in God's eye what in God's eye he is —
> Chríst — for Christ plays in ten thousand places,
> Lovely in limbs, and lovely in eyes not his
> To the Father through the features of men's faces.

This is the vision of justice which renders unto each the love that is due. Augustine reflects on the nature of love as a coda to his discussion of justice in Book 8. "Now love means someone loving and something loved with love." Love is "a kind of life coupling or trying to couple together two things, namely love and what is being loved." Lover, beloved, love. Three in one. Unequal in nature—the two human persons loving one another are not equal to the love that is God—but equalized in form by the love that is both *forma servi* and *forma dei*.

In the inward turn that is *On the Trinity* Book 8, Augustine has given us a logical, theological, and anthropological triad. Love is a unity of substance and relation. But as he notes in closing, he steps back from the propositional status of lover, beloved, love. He has trained the reader's mind for the encounter with justice in love—not the mere possession of knowledge, but the encounter with Christ's justicing in the *forma servi*, and so prompting the reader's own harmonious adjustment to the form of justice. We have not yet found what we are looking for, says Augustine, but we have "found where to look for it." It is as though we have been finding "a place where something has to be looked for .... Thus, we have said enough to provide ourselves as it were with the frame of a kind of warp on which we can weave what remains to be said" (TR 8.5.14, p. 255).

That is, the subsequent Trinitarian psychological analysis and discussions of the human image are woven upon the frame composed of justice and love. In his training of the mind, Augustine has distinguished the fabric from the frame. *Ius* and *lex* are woven within and therefore viewed with respect to justice and love. Action is ordered to obedience to justice and love, and not to power. This frame has both individual and cosmic resonance.

For, Augustine says, we were justly permitted to be handed over to the power of the devil, though we remained under God's legal jurisdiction. Through our sin, Satan acquired a right (*ius*) over us. In this formulation, Augustine squares his own language of nature and condition with the legal language of St. Paul's discussion of sin. But the cosmic context is not between alternate powers, as in Manichean and other forms of dualism. God is all-powerful, and the devil cannot compete. The contest is between power and justice.

> But the devil would have to be overcome not by God's power but by his justice. What after all could be more powerful than the all-powerful, or what creature's power could compare with the creator's? The essential flaw of the devil's perversion made him a lover of power and a deserter and assailant of justice,

which means that men imitate him all the more thoroughly the more they neglect or even detest justice and studiously devote themselves to power, rejoicing at the possession of it or inflamed with the desire for it. So it pleased God to deliver man from the devil's authority by beating him at the justice game, not the power game, so that men too might imitate Christ by seeking to beat the devil at the justice game, not the power game. Not that power is to be shunned as something bad, but that the right order must be preserved which puts justice first. How much power in any case can mortals have? (TR 13.4.17, p. 356)

Our sin is to desert justice in favor of power. Power is finite. Justice is infinite. "Let mortals hold on to justice; power will be given to them when they are immortal. Compared with this, the power of those men who are called powerful on earth is shown to be ridiculous weakness" (TR 13.4.17, p. 356). Our healing in this life is not in the possession of power but the restoration of justice. In being crucified, Christ did not lack power, but subordinated his power to justice. By contrast, in our sinful condition we seek the power to do what we will, but not the power over ourselves to will justly.

Satan, then, is not overcome or bought off. In killing Christ as *forma servi*, he punished unjustly and so loses his jurisdiction; through the misuse of his power, he loses the right to his power, and condemns himself according to the law. The same is true of humans who abuse their power.

Additionally, the Incarnation abolishes another pernicious dualism—that of soul and body. By becoming human flesh and yet not sinning, Christ reminds us that our problem is not physical but spiritual. The power over the body derives from the justice of the spirit. From the Incarnation, man learns that the wound of pride can be healed and that our infirmity can be transposed to obedience (TR 13.4.21-22, pp. 359–61).

Augustine's shifting of the field of battle from power to justice comes in the crescendo of Book 13, leading to the final formal finale of Book 14 (as distinct from the poetic epilogue which is Book 15). The discussion in Book 13 was framed as an exploration of knowledge (*scientia*). Book 14 shifts to an exploration of wisdom (*sapientia*). Knowledge is bound to virtue; wisdom is bound to worship. "God himself is supreme wisdom; but the worship of God is men's wisdom" where wisdom is defined philosophically as "the knowledge of things human and divine" (TR 14.1.1-3, pp. 370, 371). The shift from power to love takes place within the movement from knowing to loving to praising.

Again, Augustine is careful to identify the frame of the inquiry. "Faith is not what one believes but what one believes with" (TR 14.3.11, p. 380). The virtues by themselves are not enough; they help us to learn to be dependent upon God's grace. And under the grace of eternity, prudence, courage, and moderation will pass away, but justice will remain, because justice is being subject to the divine nature. In holding the persistence of justice through both *scientia* and *sapientia*, Augustine shows justice comprising the other three virtues (unlike his treatment in earlier works). Learning is a kind of presence to oneself, while vice is a form of wrongful self-forgetfulness. That is, we become most present to ourselves when we become conscious of or remember the justice to which we were born (TR 14.3.12-14, pp. 380–382).

For this reason, Augustine can note that law (*ius*) without consciousness or memory is not efficacious. Justice is both a reminder of the truth and a formation to the truth. The image of man, then, is the image of justice. God reforms the deformity which we inflicted on ourselves. "But by sinning man lost justice and the holiness of truth, and thus the image became deformed and dissolved; he gets those qualities back when he is reformed and renovated" (TR 14.4.21-14.5.22, pp. 386–89). This image of justice comes to perfection only in the complete vision of God in eternity. In this life, we bear the image in faith and hope. The pilgrim navigates his progress through a puzzling reflection in a mirror (TR 14.5.24-25, pp. 390, 391).

In this way, Augustine concludes the formal part of his argument in *On the Trinity* on a note of *aporeia*. We see through a glass darkly the image of justice and so are reflective of or formed by that image with greater or lesser clarity. Plotinus speaks of polishing the mirror of our souls with philosophy (understood as a spiritual exercise, à la Pierre Hadot). When we think of an ancient mirror as pounded and burnished metal or primitive glass, the metaphor becomes even more striking as we think of St. Paul's and Augustine's use of it. We are, as pilgrims, smoothing out the wrinkled tin foil of our souls so as to reflect more accurately the divine light.

Theologically, justification for Augustine is literally that: justifying in the sense of craftsmanship—aligning to a measure. Justification is not a payment of debt (on the contrary, it is the removal of Satan's power of jurisdiction), nor is it a blood sacrifice of atonement or satisfaction. For Augustine, Christ's death is not substitutionary. Christ's death is a sacrament and example, a reframing of the fabric of human life on the crossbeams of justice and love. In an echo of *On the Literal Interpretation of Genesis* (6.24.35), Augustine writes in *On the Trinity* Book 4 that our original justice will be restored and elevated to a higher perfection in heaven. In sin, we suffer both physical and spiritual death.

> To balance the double death of ours the savior paid in his single one, and to achieve each resurrection of ours he pre-enacted and presented his one and only by way of sacrament and by way of model (*in sacramento et exemplo*); he harmonized with each part of us by becoming in that flesh the sacrament for the inner man and the model for the outer one. (TR 4.1.6, p. 156)

This balance is a kind of "curative accord or symmetry"—not a bending or covering but a restoration or reformation by way of completion, a filling in of the gaps to achieve an integral whole (TR 4.1.5-6, pp. 155–157). Christ here is Mediator, not redeemer or savior.

By sacrament and example Christ's death "justices"—it enacts justice as wholeness, or completion. One can sense the pulse of excitement in Augustine's prose even in translation:

> By nature we are not God; by nature we are men; by sin we are not just. So God became a just man to intercede with God for sinful man. The sinner did not match the just, but man did match man. So he applied to us the similarity of his humanity to take away the dissimilarity of our iniquity, and becoming a partaker of our mortality he made us partakers of his divinity. It was surely right that the death of the sinner issuing from the stern necessity of condemnation should be undone by the death of the just man issuing from the voluntary freedom of mercy, his single matching our double.
>
> This match—or agreement or concord or consonance or whatever the right word is for the proportion of one to two—is of enormous importance in every construction or interlock (*coaptatio*)—that is the word I want—of creation. What I mean by this interlock, it has just occurred to me, is what the Greeks call *harmonia*. This is not the place to show the far-reaching importance of the consonant proportion of the single to the double. It is found extensively in us, and is so naturally ingrained

in us (and who by, if not by him who created us?), that even the unskilled feel it whether singing themselves or listening to others. It is what makes concord between high-pitched and deep voices, and if anyone strays discordantly away from it, it is not our knowledge, which many lack, but our very sense of hearing that is painfully offended. To explain it would require a long lecture; but anyone who knows how can demonstrate it to our ears with a tuning string, or tonometer.

As for our present concern, what has to be explained as far as God permits is how the single of our Lord Jesus Christ matches our double, and in some fashion enters into a harmony of salvation (*salus*) with it. (TR 4.1.4-5, p. 155)

The immediacy of Augustine's insight is palpable, and to observe his grasping for the right word is to see a powerful mind at work. Indeed, Augustine seems to have coined the word *coaptatio*, which Hill translates as "interlock," noting that the Greek *harmonia* is more related to a carpenter's joint or fastener or clamp than it is to music. In this sense, the son of the carpenter completes our dovetail joint, two becoming one, fingers intertwined in an inseparable unity.

But Augustine's own description refers to music—in theory and in practice (cf. CG 22.24.4, LG 10.21, and MS 6.14.47). The musical theory we can best understand in terms of the octave, and the numerical relation of other chordal structures. This is "the consonate proportion of the single to the double": Christ strikes the note that brings harmony out of discord, turning what is dissonant into the beauty of consonance. Augustine supplies an elaborate theory of numbers in *On the Trinity* 4.2.7-12 as a way of illustrating the point. But without the mathematics we understand in practice "what makes concord between high-pitched and deep voices"; we might note in passing that Cicero (*Tusculan Disputations* 1.10.19) uses "intention" to describe the tuning of the soul. Not only does Christ sound the note of concord (*sacramento*) but he becomes the key to which the voice of creation are returned. This harmony, or harmonizing, is the restoration of health (*salus*) to the created order, and the elevation of the symphony of creation to a higher order, anticipated in time by faith, experienced in heaven with immediacy.

Augustine discusses this symphony of justice in terms of both ontological and moral unity. "Just as Father and Son are one not only by equality of substance but also by identity of will, so these men, for whom the Son is mediator with God, might be one not only by being of the same nature, but also by being bound in the fellowship of the same love." When we are "made one in the one just one" we are "fused somehow into one spirit in the furnace of charity," Augustine writes (TR 4.2.11-12, pp. 160, 161). Our natures are restored but our loves are elevated to a different plane. And this harmony of wills echoes with sympathetic vibrations the catalog of peace of *City of God* Book 19. Christ's "sacrifice of peace" not only restores our original justice but also restores the cosmic *ius* by releasing us from the just bondage to Satan (TR 4.3.17, p. 165). In some sense, the harmonization of Christ's justice is both decisive in time, in the *forma servi*, and ongoing, in the *forma dei*—a continuing musical improvisation in response to human action in the course of time, a creative work of reconciliation or consonance understood as the restoration of the regularity of order to a world at once made beautiful by human freedom and compromised by it.

We are, in the end, "in that tavern to which that Samaritan brought the man he found half-dead from the many wounds inflicted on him by robbers." In the course of the explanation of the Trinity, the reader's mind has worked hard, his eyes have seen marvelous things, and the labor is difficult and the attention is undeveloped (TR 15, Epil. 50, p. 435). We are pilgrims wounded by sin but in the care of Christ and Church, traveling toward the promised land we have glimpsed, but which, in time, we shall not enter.

Where, then, is the beauty in suffering? Christ's suffering was unjust, and in this injustice Satan's just punishment of our sinfulness was delegitimized. But we suffer justly, Augustine maintains in a difficult teaching, for suffering is the natural consequence either of our disobedience to the law's command or to the disorder of our loves in response to suffering that is imposed by others unjustly. We can be unjust in both our acts and in our response to acts that impinge upon us. By example, Christ teaches us that it is possible to suffer unjustly and to overcome that injustice with love, by resisting the power game.

There are two responses to injustice and suffering: power and love. Power yields destruction; love bears fruit. In loving despite unjust suffering, we do not necessarily heal or repair the wound, but we do help complete and so give shape to a new form. That is, Augustine's vision is not compensatory—what possible compensation could there be for abject suffering? Nor is Augustine's a vision of a return to the status quo ante. Christ as Mediator (or moderator, modulator in musical terms) takes suffering and elevates being in the course of time to a higher completion. A deep scratch in the surface of a wooden table cannot be repaired, but it can be polished to a new and rich radiance, fuller in character and texture for the damage it has received, the bearer of a story turned from darkness to light.

Augustine's treatment of Christ's crucifixion in *On the Trinity* is understandably clinical and philosophical, so much so that it might seem almost mathematically arid. Augustine's appeal is not to Christ's pain—we are not to love justice from guilt or sympathy for Christ's suffering. The challenge is to see in the aesthetic beauty of the arrangements of disparate parts the full warmth of the human heart. How are we to put together the intellectual apprehension of justice as completeness in love with the lived experience of human suffering?

The fullest of Augustine's laments are not lacking in pathos, however. Quite the contrary. We see in *Confessions* the most profound and poetic discussions of his own suffering. And as is so often the case with Augustine, we see him wrestling with his own experience and wrestling with the meaning of that experience as a way of comprehending the order of things in time. *Confessions* is indeed a narrative about the quest for love and truth that fully satisfies. But the inverse of that story, the negative space as it were created by that narrative, is the quest to escape suffering. At the philosophical and theological level, the search for love and truth operates largely on the level of head and heart. But the pulse of the emotions runs strong, and even as Augustine uses the language of desire to analyze his restlessness, he recognizes the full power of the emotions—joy, fear, sorrow.

There are four attachments in the *Confessions* narrative which give rise to the most profound suffering: literature, an unnamed friend, his similarly unnamed mistress, and his mother. These four attachments provide an anatomy, as it were, of the wounds of the arrow of beauty.

The first is what we might term "vicarious suffering." When we see a good stage play, or read of Dido's desolation and suicide, why does the suffering of the character delight us? We know that their suffering is not real, and if we were to encounter such misfortunes in our own lives outside of the stage or text, the suffering would prompt distress not delight. We want to be happy, and yet what is the happiness that we have when we love imaginary tears and sorrow? Augustine does not offer us Aristotelian explanations of catharsis; vicarious suffering is not a purging of pity and fear. We do not love suffering, Augustine contends, but we want to have compassion: "is it that, while no one wants to be miserable, one still does want to have compassion, and, since one cannot feel compassion without feeling suffering, this and this alone is the reason why sufferings are loved?" (CF 3.2, p. 53). Augustine's answer is only an implied affirmative, but his discussion frames two quite distinct objects of compassion. The anatomy of suffering is inseparable from the analysis of compassion. What are the experiences which give rise to true compassion?

The false compassion is that which turns us inward, prompting a delight in our own sadness which blinds us to the beauty of the whole. This is the sadness which we possess and which in turn possesses us. Such sorrow is an infected wound, the scratching of which provides temporary relief but no lasting solace. "But I poor wretch, at that time loved to feel sad and went looking for something to feel sad about" (CF 3.2, p. 54). His objects were stage plays and friendships. The friendships of Book 3 are generally seen as surreptitious, lustful encounters, and indeed Augustine portrays them that way. These are superficial friendships of physical pleasure and spiritual pain. The suffering is not willed, but a by-product of the restless, misplaced love. Like the stage plays, these friendships are imaginary, acted out, and reinforced by a sense of true compassion about an unworthy object. These imaginary sorrows "had, as it were, the effect of scratching the surface of my skin. And, as happens after the scratching of poisoned nails, what came next were feverish swellings, abscesses, and running sores. Such was the life I led" (CF 3.2, pp. 54, 55).

In contrast to the scratching of personal sorrow, Augustine asks whether our compassion is directed toward a worthy object. "Is compassion, then, to be cast out? Certainly not. We must therefore allow ourselves to love sufferings. But beware of uncleanness, my soul" (CF 3.2, pp. 53, 54). Compassion, Augustine says, is more properly addressed toward the moral state, not the hardship that comes from the lack of an inordinate pleasure. This form of compassion does not give one pleasure, and in this is true compassion—a suffering with.

This certainly is a truer form of compassion, but the pain in it does not give me pleasure. To feel grief for another's misery is a sign and work of charity and is therefore to be commended; but it is still true that a man who is genuinely compassionate would rather that there was nothing for him to feel grief about. (CF 3.2, p. 54)

Only an evil will would wish there to be suffering so as to be able to show compassion. "Some sorrow, therefore, may be approved of, but none loved. For this, Lord God, is your way. You are wounded by no sorrow, yet you love souls far more deeply than we can, and your compassion is more lasting and indestructible than ours" (CF 3.2, p. 54). The divine compassion is prompted by love alone, not by the wound of suffering.

Augustine's discussion of vicarious suffering presents us with this choice—do we love suffering or souls? We might distinguish, then, between two forms of compassion: selfish compassion (we suffer with and for ourselves) and soulful compassion (we suffer with and for another). Correspondingly, there are two forms of suffering: suffering from the lack of pleasure and suffering from the lack of good. Why do we love the suffering that is bad for our souls? This love springs, Augustine says, "from the lust of power, the lust of the eye, the lust of feeling—sometimes from one of these, sometimes from two, sometimes from all three." Those who act "wickedly against their own souls ... take pleasure in the collapse of the standards of human society and brazenly set up, according to their own likes and dislikes, their private combinations or factions." In forsaking the fountain of life, we injure ourselves by asserting "the private and arrogant self-will which falsely attributes unity to a part and loves it." In private, selfish compassion we raise against God "the standard of an unreal liberty" and, in desire for more, risk the loss of everything by setting our love more upon our own private good "against the Three and the Seven, the psaltery of ten strings, your Ten Commandments, O God most high and sweet" (CF 3.8, p. 64).

Vicarious suffering substitutes the sour for the sweet in a perverse, selfish compassion which collapses into the private at the expense of a common good. Such suffering embraces the part, not the whole, and in possessing misery becomes misery's slave.

If vicarious suffering has as its object imagination relationships—those of the fictions of literature or the fictions of friendship—the immediate suffering of more genuine friendship marks a deeper pain. The deaths of Augustine's unnamed friend and of Augustine's mother, Monnica, and his separation from his longtime mistress, the unnamed mother of his son, Adeodatus, touch Augustine to the core, and force a deeper analysis of suffering. There, Augustine struggles to come to terms with the strange ways in which the suffering of real misfortune brings with it a kind of joy.

Augustine describes his short-lived but deep friendship of nine months as "a friendship that was sweeter to me than all the sweetness that in this life I had ever known." This was an affair not of the body but of the soul. At his friend's death, he says,

> My heart was darkened over with sorrow, and whatever I looked at was death. My own country was a torment to me, my own home was a strange unhappiness. All those things which we had done and said together became, now that he was gone, sheer torture to me. My eyes looked for him everywhere and could not find him. (CF 4.4, pp. 74, 75)

Augustine experienced a literal and spiritual displacement. He is no longer at home, either in place or in the light of the mind's eye, in the studies which had brought them together. "I had become a great riddle to myself and I used to ask my soul why it was sad and why is disquieted me so sorely" (CF 4.4, p. 75).

And yet, in the midst of this anguish, Augustine says, "Only tears were sweet to me, and tears had taken the place of my friend in my heart's love." Why then are these tears sweet?, Augustine asks. "How is it, then, that from the bitterness of life we can pluck such fruit in mourning and weeping and sighing and lamentations?" There would seem to be in this immediate suffering a double wound—the agony of loss, and the perplexing sweetness of the agony over the agony of loss (CF 4.5, p. 75). This agony becomes a kind of rest. "I wept most bitterly, and I found repose in bitterness" (CF 4.6, p. 76).

With the passing of time and pain, Augustine says he came to see in his suffering a disoriented loss of self in his friend. He had not yet learned "how to love men as they should be loved" (CF 4.7, p. 77). That is, he had invested his love—a love of the soul to be sure—disproportionately in something mortal, one in whom he had found a second self. "For I felt that my soul and my friend's had been one soul in two bodies, and that is why I had a horror of living, because I did not want to live as a half-being" (CF 4.6, p. 76). This disorientation prompted a dislocation, and though "my heart could not flee from my heart, nor could I escape from myself," he did flee his native town of Thagaste and did escape to Carthage.

So it is that we learn that Augustine's pursuit of "unholy loves" in Carthage, with which he begins Book 3, are the rebounding loves, as it were, of the immediate suffering after his friend's death. It is the suffering of real ills that pushes him to the imaginary objects of vicarious suffering. And yet we are to understand that this love for his friend, however deep, was misplaced in the order of value.

Augustine's displacement is to have sought and found a unity in friendship without the unity of the whole of created love. That is, his friendship was only a partial wholeness; only a wholeness within a wholeness can be the place of true repose. Augustine's wholeness with his friend did not include the wholeness of their souls with God. It is the Word itself which "calls you to come back; and there is the place of peace that is imperturbable, where love cannot be forsaken unless it first forsakes" (CF 4.11, p. 80). Christ is "the Life" which "came down to us and suffered our death and destroyed death by the abundance of his own life: and he thundered, calling us to return to Him into that secret place from which He came out to us" (CF 4.13, p. 82). As the sacrament and example of justice, Christ's suffering resolves even death into the beauty of wholeness, not discounting the suffering, but completing its particularity in love.

Augustine's love for and separation from his mistress seem to follow the same pattern of immediate suffering as that of his unnamed friend. His companion of a decade and a half, Augustine's mistress was an impediment to a marriage intended to advance his career and social status. Amid a long discussion of the weariness of advancing in society, Augustine tells us only that his mistress "was torn from his side ... and my heart, which clung to her, was broken and wounded and dripping blood" (CF 4.15, pp. 132, 133). He gives us no extended meditation of suffering here, just raw pain.

Unlike the suffering at the death of his friend, which prompted deeper reflection on his own emotions and on the conception of parts and wholes, the discussion of his mistress is embedded in a twofold pattern of fragmentary love—a desire for completeness in social status, and a desire for completeness in carnal love. He continues in his pursuit of career success, advancing brilliantly both in celebrity and profound unhappiness; he finds serial lovers while, having sent his mistress away, he waits two years for his political betrothed to reach a marriageable age. And at the same time, Augustine and his friends are imagining a retreat from business, crafting plans for a philosophical commune—professionals and wives retiring in the hills above Milan to form a small, more complete society not riven by superficiality and gain. The plan was not permanently realized, though it did plant the seeds for Augustine's post-conversion retreat at Cassiciacum, and his vision of monastic community later realized in Hippo. Just as Augustine sought permanent wholeness in the love of his mortal friend, here Augustine seeks a lasting peace in the social bonds derived from networked marriages and family life, whether in broader Milanese imperial society or in an intentional community of philosophical friends.

The death of Augustine's mother, Monnica, prompts a meditation in a third category of suffering, the suffering that bears fruit. Monnica's death takes place after Augustine's decisive embrace of Christ and so Augustine finds himself differently equipped to puzzle through the suffering. He begins, "Why, then, did I feel such pain within me?" despite the fact that his mother had lived piously and died peacefully. "It was because the wound was still fresh, the wound caused by the sudden breaking off of our old way of living together in such sweet affection" (CF 9.12, p. 204). Here Augustine laments not only the passing away of his mother but his attachment to a familiar way of life. The attachments themselves are not inordinate—he is lamenting the loss of genuine goods which necessarily come to be and pass away in time. Beyond his struggle to find a supplemental good, Augustine grieves at his grief. Whereas with the death of his friend and his separation from his mistress Augustine sought to understand his tears, here he seeks to understand his failure to cry. He does not cry initially, and instead takes refuge in philosophical conversation with his friends, who marvel at his self-control. "So I was using truth as a kind of fomentation to dull my torture," a torture not apparent to his friends. "I knew well enough what I was crushing down in my heart. And I was deeply vexed that these human feelings should have such power over me—though in the proper order and lot of the human conditions these things must be—and I grieved at my grief with a new grief and so was consumed with a double sorrow" (CF 9.12, p. 205).

Previously Augustine had come to see that his grief was the product of self-deception, of having pursued lesser goods as though they were greater goods. Here his double grief is of the loss of a genuine good, and grief at the grief of his loss. In this Augustine ultimately comes to see "how strong is the bond of all habit, even upon a soul which is no longer nourished by deceiving words" (CF 9.12, p. 206). And so, finally, Augustine finds himself shedding tears at last for his mother and for himself, making tears, he says, "a pillow for my heart, and my heart rested in them" (CF 9.12, pp. 206, 207).

But after the healing of his heart, Augustine finds himself shedding "tears of a very different sort for your handmaid," tears at the angers laid bare, by contrast, the angers that threaten those without Monnica's faith and piety (CF 9.13, p. 207). Foremost among Monnica's virtues, Augustine notes, were her patient obedience and her capacity to recognize when to respond with loving reason. She demonstrated this most prominently with her unfaithful and violent tempered husband, Patricius, but Augustine tells us that Monnica's perspicacity spared her from the apparently common domestic physical abuse suffered by her peers. Augustine's father never hit Monnica, he says, because she did not contradict him when he was angry, but waited for more opportune moments to explain her reasoning (CF 9.9, p. 198).

The example might alarm the contemporary mind, but the principle is consistent with Augustine's description of the work of Christ—to contradict power not with power but with reasoned justice, bending the dissonance of sin to a more perfect harmony. This is obedience "with patience bringing forth fruit," quoting scripture, suffering (patience from *patientia < passio*) which turns a wound into wholeness (CF 9.13, p. 208). There is not beauty in suffering itself, but when the light of justice shines through suffering, piercing the shadows of power, beauty shines through with a patience that bears fruit.

In this, both Christ's suffering and our own pierce the wounds of created beauty and raise it to a greater perfection. This is the freely creative act, not to resist power with power, but to restore and reconcile the darkness of power to the wholeness of justice, to deploy the freedom of patience as the created complement to a created nature not compromised by the misuse of human freedom. The patience which brings forth fruit is the improvisational, creative work of reconciliation understood as the restoration— graced by Christ's sacrament and in imitation of his example—of the regularity and wholeness of the created order.

6

The Music of the Word

Poetry healed Augustine's wounded heart. As he grieved for the death of his mother, and grieved over his grief, he sought a remedy. Philosophical conversation with friends kept his public face strong, but was not balm for the inner reaches of his soul. Philology and physiology likewise fell short—Augustine tells us without any hint of irony that he went to the baths for healing, because he had read that the Latin word for bath (*balneum*) derived from the Greek *balaneion*, meaning "something that drives sadness from the mind" (CF 9.12, p. 206). This, too, had no effect. His moment of healing, he says, comes upon awaking from a good night's sleep and recalling in bed some verses written by Ambrose:

> Creator Thou of everything
> Director of the circling poles
> Clothing the clay in lovely light
> And giving night the grace of sleep,
>
> That peace may fall on loosened limbs
> To make them strong for work again,
> To raise and soothe the tired mind
> And free the anxious from their care. (CF 9.12, p. 206)

It is likely that these Ambrosian verses were also sung as a hymn in Milan. It is the music of the word that shifts Augustine's soul to the contemplation not of his loss, but of his mother's holiness. This moment, which parallels in Book 9 Augustine's mystical vision with his mother on the balcony at Ostia, is not any less of a conversion, a turning, than the many other conversions which shower the

Confessions. Indeed, the arc of *Confessions* 1 to 9 is Augustine's shift from corporeal thinking to incorporeal thinking, from the propositions of the mind to the dispositions of the heart, and now (we see) from philosophy to poetry.

Ambrose's words are the wordless peace which comforts Augustine's soul, the music which returns the strings of sadness to the contemplation of holiness. The music of poetry echoes here like the effect of Cicero's *Hortensius*—it shifts Augustine's disposition, alters his way of feeling. His recollection of these verses realigns his soul and, in juxtaposition to his friendly philosophical conversations, reveals the limits of philosophy itself. While philosophy may illuminate the conditions of suffering, it shows itself to be an inadequate comfort, incapable of healing the soul. Like John the Baptist, Augustine's philosophy prepares the way for and then yields to poetry, it yields to praise, that embrace of God and the order of creation in which we relinquish the need to know and find restoration in the arms of love.

Book 9 concludes with the prayer-praise of Monnica's holiness, and so sets the stage for Augustine's discussion of memory in Book 10. That is, while Augustine's concluding meditations on memory (Book 10) and time (Books 11–13) are clearly philosophical, they are to be read through the lens of poetry. How do words and silences prompt resonances which connect us to the very core of creation?

Viewing Books 1–9 of *Confessions* as a structural sub-unit, Augustine's turn to poetry at the end of Book 9 may be seen as the redemption of poetry condemned at the end of Book 1. With echoes of Plato's critique of poetry in *The Republic*, Augustine in Book 1 decries how he and his fellow students "were forced to go wandering ourselves in the tracks of poetic fictions," turning poetry into prose for declamation and using both poetry and prose for seduction and deceit (CF 1.17, p. 35). The art rejected in Book 1 for its role in the domination of others by power of words is turned, in Book 9, to a vehicle of loving humility in the praise of God's justice. *Deus creator omnium*. The substance of Augustine's praise of Monnica is not her mechanical obedience to an abstract code of piety, but the fittingness and aptness of her words and gestures to each circumstance, however threatening. That is, Augustine praises the poetry of her life in being able, like Christ, to complete the line of every situation with the right word.

Poetry, then, becomes the motif for understanding the graced completion of created nature, the rendering of what is just, in the sense of what is fitting, for each place and time. Poetry becomes not only the completion of philosophy in prayer, but the expression of the law as a pedagogical principle.

Goodness, Augustine tells us in *Confessions* Book 3, makes its judgment not from convention "but from the most right and undeviating law of God almighty." The law is the same everywhere, but "the customs of different times and places are formed as is right for those times and those places." To condemn Abraham, Isaac, Moses, or David for practice permitted in their day but forbidden in our own, says Augustine, "is a mark of ignorance, for it is to judge merely out of man's judgment and to measure the whole moral structure of the human race by one's own particular and partial standard of morality." It is to impose, across time, a private morality upon a public practice (CF 3.7, p. 61).

The immediate context of Augustine's discussion here is his resistance to rigid Manichean doctrine and his youthful ignorance of what it is to be made "after the image of God." Against the Manichees' mechanistic materialism and the dualistic clash of good and evil, Augustine safeguards the possibilities of human creativity and variation within the overarching principle of natural law. Measure does not mean uniformity, but rather fittingness and proportionality. We would not complain if we put a shin guard on the head or a helmet on the foot. We understand that one servant has proprietary roles within the house that are not permitted to others. That which is allowed behind the stables is not permitted in the dining room. Or "as if one should be indignant that in one house and one family there is not exactly the same system of distribution to everyone." What is true of space is true also of time, Augustine avers. The law permits and reflects different creative responses to time and place, and yet "both in the past and in the present it is the same goodness to which obedience is due" (CF 3.7, p. 61).

Augustine's position is not one of moral relativism but a classic natural law position which holds the creative variation of human law appropriate to time and circumstance as an expression of natural and eternal law. "Does this mean that justice is something which changes and varies? No, it does not; but the times, over which Justice presides, do not pass by evenly; for they are times." Human beings, with their necessarily limited experience in time, cannot find in other times and places "the same relations of cause and effect" which they experience in their own time and place (CF

3.7, p. 62). The creative possibilities of our own age obscure the creative responses to circumstances of other ages.

Poetry, for Augustine, holds the key:

> For instance, when I wrote poetry, I was not allowed to use every kind of foot wherever I liked; different feet had to be used in different meters, and even in the same meter one could not use the same foot in every part of the line. Yet the art of poetry, in accordance with which I wrote, did not have different principles for different occasions; it comprised all the rules together in itself. And still I could not see that the rule of righteousness, followed by these good and holy men, comprised, in a much more lofty and sublime sense, all its precepts together, and that in itself it never varied at all, although at various times, instead of prescribing everything at once, it laid down rules and principles proper for each occasion. (CF 3.7, p. 62)

The rules of law and custom, like the rules of poetry, are not to be contravened simply for "lawless pleasure." For the rule orients the parts to the whole. Where the whole of society is at odds with the wholeness of God's creation, however, God, "The Ruler of all creation is to be obeyed" (CF 3.8, p. 63).

At the end of *Confessions* Book 3, Augustine tells us of his mother's dream, in which she is standing on a kind of wooden ruler. In the dream, Augustine comes to be standing with his mother on the wooden ruler, a sign (which he resists at the time) of his eventual conversion (CF 3.11, pp. 66, 67). The image is a primitive one, but forces consideration of the broader question—by what are we ruled? By what are we measured? The poetry of law allows us to engage the questions simultaneously, for the rules and measure of poetry (or of music) provide restrictive but non-determinative frameworks. As with poetry or music, laws—both natural and customary—are design constraints which breed, indeed demand, creativity.

Poetry and music are arts which take place in time. The wholeness of God's countenance illuminates what comes to be and passes away.

> Turn us, O God of hosts, show us thy countenance and we shall be whole. For wherever man's soul turns, except toward you, it is fixed to sorrows, even if it fixes itself on things of beauty

outside you and outside itself. These things of beauty would have no existence at all unless they were from you. They rise and set; in their rising they begin, as it were, to exist; they develop so as to reach their perfection, and after that they grow old and die; not all grow old, but all die. So, when they rise and reach their way into existence, the quicker they are to grow in to being, the more they hurry toward ceasing to be. That is their law. So much you have given them, namely to be parts of a structure in which the parts are not all in existence at the same time; instead, by fading and replacing each other, they all together constitute the universe of which they are parts. Our own speech, too, which is constructed out of meaningful sounds, follows the same principles. There could never be a complete sentence unless one word, as soon as the syllables had been sounded, ceased to be in order to make room for the next. In these things let my soul praise you, God, creator of all things, yet let it not be stuck and glued too close to them in love through the sense of the body. For these things go along their path toward nonexistence, and they tear and wound the soul with terrible longings, since the soul itself desires to be and to find rest in what it loves. But in those things there is no place to rest, since they do not stay. They pass away and no one can follow them with his bodily senses. Nor can anyone grasp them tight even while they are present and in front of him. (CF 4.10, pp. 79, 80)

The law of temporal things is that they fade and replace each other. The beauty of the whole is dependent upon the impermanence of the parts, and correspondingly the beauty of the parts can only be seen as shimmering reflections of the light of the beauty of the whole. Seen in isolation, the parts of space and time wound us in their passage to non-existence. Seen as parts of a composite whole, they are lenses magnifying the brilliant light of creation and cast us into the rest that can only be found in God's permanence.

The created order is like a poem in which syllables sound and dissipate, words are separated by silences, each sound has its meaning only when it ceases to sound and in the fullness of the symphony of other sounds which came before and which will come after. Each must make room for the next in the linear flow of time. In so doing, they not only create space for succeeding beauty, but contribute to the texture and color of meaning, like the lower layers of paint upon which the artist builds his final image. At the same time, each sound continues to echo in its silence, having been a response to previous and an inspiration to subsequent sounds.

To turn from the perception of the partial, the private, to the whole, to see the private in the context of the whole, is to come to perceive the whole sentence of creation in its entirety. The challenge, then, is not to accommodate oneself to the necessity of change, but to delight in change in the fullness of its beauty, even in things passing away, to "have the greater pleasure of perceiving the entirety of things."

> For these words we speak are perceived by you through your bodily sense, and you certainly do not want to hear the same syllables forever; you want them to pass away so that others may come and so that you may hear the whole sentence. And this is always the case when one thing is made up of many parts and all the parts do not exist together at the same time. To perceive all the parts together at once would give more pleasure than to perceive each individual part separately. But far better than these is He who made all things, and He is our God. And He does not pass away, because there is nothing to take His place. (CF 4.11, pp. 80, 81)

Augustine's reflections on his love of the "lower beauties" of his youth prompted him to ask his friends the following question: "Do we love anything except what is beautiful? What, then, is the beautiful? And what is beauty? What is it that attracts us and wins our affection for the things we love?" We are drawn, he says, to the grace and beauty in that which we love, where "one sort of beauty ... comes from a thing constituting a whole, and another sort of grace ... comes from the right and apt relationship of one thing to another." That is, that which draws our love has an integrity or wholeness in itself, and a grace in its relationship to the things around it (CF 4.13, pp. 82, 83). It is the law that regulates both internal integrity (with respect to a thing's created nature) and its complementarity to that around it (with respect to its adaptability in relationship to other created natures). And so Augustine praises God, "the one alone from whom is every manner of form, you, most beautiful, the creator of beauty in all things, you who by your law lay down for all things the rule" (CF 1.6, p. 24).

Beauty, it would seem, consists in maintaining a natural integrity while adapting graciously and gracefully to those natures around us. Such is a constant, virtuosic improvisation, as time and place change around us and change us. What beauty is for Augustine, excellence (*arête*) is for Aristotle: to do the right thing, in the right way, at the right time, for the right reason, to the right person. And because beauty has an internal dimension (integrity) and an external direction (fittingness), beauty is never static; it is almost infinitely dynamic. The beautiful and the fitting are the arts of equilibrium, the constant adjustments of stability which, while always in motion, are anchored at rest.

Augustine tells us that in his youth he wrote two or three books on "The Beautiful and the Fitting." He cannot remember: "I no longer have the books. Somehow or other they have disappeared" (CF 4.13, p. 83). He reveals that he enjoyed his mediations and thought the work "very good." He dedicated the work to a famous orator, Hiereus, whom he admired but had never met. But Hiereus possessed qualities that Augustine himself would have liked to possess. The books that have gone missing, then, serve two purposes for Augustine's narrative in *Confessions* Book 4: to remind us of our vanity, wanting recognition from others rather than God; and to caution against too material a notion of beauty.

Augustine finds fault in his analysis for drawing exclusively on corporeal examples, but the structure of his thinking about the beautiful and the fitting dovetails, interlocks, with his conception of physical and spiritual peace.

> As I wrote them I turned over in my mind all those corporeal fictions which made such a noise that the ears of my heart were deafened. Yet, sweet truth, I was straining these ears to try to hear you inner melody, as I meditated upon "The Beautiful and the Fitting" and I longed to stand and hear you and rejoice with joy at the voice of the bridegroom; but I could not. (CF 4.15, pp. 86, 87)

The voices of his own pride and error drowned out the music of the word.

It is not clear whether Augustine lost or destroyed this early work, which he says he wrote at the age of 26 or 27. What is clear is that the beautiful and the fitting, conceived in the fullness of material and immaterial form, remained an anchoring framework for his thinking. One might see the whole of *Confessions* as the narration of coming to understand the beautiful in relation to God and the fitting in relation to neighbor and creation over time.

To be beautiful is to have a loving relationship toward change and the mystery of time. As we have seen, this loving relationship toward change requires coming to terms with mortality—others' mortality and one's own—not loving death, but placing the beauty of those we love and want to hold on to in relationship to the grace of what is appropriate to the whole. The question, What is beauty? also asks the question, What is time? for time is the medium of change in which we measure a standard of value.

How do we measure time? Once again, it is the music of poetry that provides the touchstone. When a voice is speaking, "What we measure is the space between a beginning and an end." When we measure the length of a poetic line, we measure the relative length of the syllables. The example Augustine proposes is the opening line of St. Ambrose's hymn: *Deus creator omnium*. The line contains eight syllables, alternately long and short, and one must cease for the other to begin. Similarly, there must be a silence, however brief, between each syllable for the syllables to sound distinctly. Each space or silence between syllables has its own quality and dimensionality, its own character. "Therefore what I am meaning is not the syllables themselves (they no longer exist) but something in my memory which remain there fixed" (CF 11.27, pp. 280, 281).

It is no accident that Augustine chooses Ambrose's *Deus creator omnium*. For what do we measure in memory, but creation itself and its divine spark? We measure time in time. When we imagine the coming to be and passing away of created things in the course of time, we remember the poem of creation which takes shape even as we recite our small part in it.

> Suppose I am about to recite a psalm which I know. Before I begin, my expectation (or "looking forward") is extended over the whole psalm. But once I have begun, whatever I pluck off from it and let fall into the past enters the province of my memory (or "looking back at"). So the life of this action of mine is extended in two directions—toward my memory, as regards what I have recited, and toward my expectation, as regards what I am about to recite. But all the time my attention (my "looking at") is present and through it what was future passes on its way to become past. And as I proceed

further and further with my recitation, so the expectation grows shorter and the memory grows longer, until all the expectation is finished at the point when the whole of this action is over and has passed into the memory. And what is true of the whole psalm is also true of every part of the psalm and of every syllable in it. The same holds good for any longer action, of which the psalm may be only a part. It is true also of the whole of a man's life, of which all of his actions are parts. And it is true of the whole history of humanity, of which the lives of all men are parts. (CF 11.28, p. 282)

What follows in *Confessions* Books 12 and 13 is a further explication of Genesis' account of creation, not unlike that we have seen in *On the Literal Interpretation of Genesis*. Similarities and differences between the two (and other of Augustine's) accounts of Genesis need not concern us here. It is enough to note the structure of *Confessions*: Augustine begins with reflections on himself, and on the perils of corporeal thinking, and ends with reflections on God and creation, and the challenges of incorporeal, imageless thinking. How do we understand the integrity of God apart from our own experience of time and space, especially when, as Augustine says, we experience life as a scattered psalm, "a kind of distraction and dispersal"? (CF 11.29, p. 283). And how do we grasp "that formless matter which you had created without beauty and form" which comes to be that "from which you were to make this beautiful world"? (CF 12.4, pp. 286, 287). Augustine's meditation on his own life is an explanation of how that which has less form may come to have more form. Just as every created being has its own measure, number, and weight with respect to its being in space, so too it has its discrete form in time also, or it would admit of no temporal variation, no change. "For where there is no variety of motion, there is no time, and there can be no variety where there is no definition of form" (CF 12.11, p. 292).

Our formation can be measured only with respect to our definition in time and space, which is to say our ever-changing restlessness in pursuit of God's changeless rest. Our own habits of self-dispersal, scattering ourselves and our desires, press against our recollection of the tranquility of resting in the divine. Our distraction longs to be gathered into the wholeness of time and space.

Whereas we create always with pre-existent matter, less or more formed, God creates ex nihilo. Again, music provides the analogy.

> When a tune is sung, the sound of it is heard; we do not first have an unformed sound and later a sound that is shaped into a song. Each sound, just as it is made, passes away, and you can find nothing that you can call back again and shape by art, and thus the tune has its being in the sound and the sound of the tune is the matter of the tune. And this matter receives a form so that it may become a tune. And therefore, as I said, the matter of the sound is prior to the form of the tune—not prior in the sense of having the power to make it, for sound is not the composer of tunes, it is merely supplied by the body to the mind of the singer for him to use in making a song; nor is it prior in time, for it is uttered simultaneously with the tune; nor it is it prior in choice, for a sound is not better than a tune, since a tune is not only a sound, but a beautiful sound. But it is prior in origin, because a tune is not given form in order to become a sound, whereas a sound is given form in order to become a tune. (CF 12.29, p. 312)

From this we may begin, Augustine says, to understand how matter and form come to be simultaneously in the creation of heaven and earth; not material, not efficient, but formal causality embraces the simultaneity of creation. This is the music of the creative word which shines forth in time and space with the tranquility of order. It is this vision that allows us to "use the law lawfully, the end of the commandment, pure charity" (CF 12.30, p. 313).

Our voices in the choir of the music of the word depend upon the order of the law, and yet to use the law lawfully—not as an end in itself but as a means to an end—is to sing with love.

> Give yourself to me, my God, and give yourself back to me. See, I love, and if my love is too little, I would love more. I cannot measure it so as to know how much my love falls short of what is enough for my life to run to your embrace and never be turned away until it is hidden in the hidden place of Thy presence. (CF 13.8, p. 321)

Augustine's text begins to sing its final climax.

> In your gift we rest; there we enjoy you. Our rest is our place. Love lifts us up to it, and your good spirit raises our lowness from the gates of death. In your good pleasure is our peace. A body tends to go of its own weight to its own place, not necessarily

downward toward the bottom, but to its own place. Fire tends to rise upward; a stone falls downward. Things are moved by their own weights and go toward their proper places. If you put oil underneath water it will rise above the level of the water; if you pour water on top of oil, it will sink below the oil; things are moved by their own weights and go to their proper places. When at all out of their place, they become restless; put them back in order and they we be at rest. My weight is my love; wherever I am carried, it is my love that carries me there. By your gift we are set on fire and are carried upward; we are red hot and we go. We ascend Thy ways that be in our heart and sing a song of degrees. We are red hot with your fire, your good fire, and we go; for we are going upward toward the peace of Jerusalem; for gladdened was I in those who said unto me, We will go up to the house of the Lord. It is there that your good pleasure will have us settled, so that we may desire nothing else but to remain there forever. (CF 13.9, pp. 321, 322)

The remainder of Book 13 is a choral hymn of and by creation. God's words are "stretched out ... like a skin" over all creation, a book which the angels

read without syllables that are spoken in time .... They read; they choose; they love; their reading is perpetual and what they read never passes away; for by choosing and by loving they read the very unchangeableness of your counsel. Their book is never closed, nor is their scroll folded up, for you yourself are their book and you are forever. (CF 13.15, pp. 326, 327)

But for mortals, the reading is periodic, the scroll often ambiguous, the words stretched thin to a breaking point so that our attention is turned from creator to created seen in the light of our own eyes, not God's. It is not of us yet to see God as God is.

We reflect the light of the divine firmament but mistake the light as our own. And yet the "tongues like as of fire" with "the word of life" beckon to us. "Run, run everywhere, holy fires, fires of beauty" (CF 13.19, pp. 331, 332). The beauty of creation, of the words of the divine book, can be understood and expressed in a multiplicity of ways. Regardless of signification, the things of creation taken individually were only good, but taken together as a whole, they are both good and very good. The same truth is expressed by all beautiful bodies. A body made up itself of members which are all beautiful is very much more beautiful than the individual members out of whose well-ordered harmony the whole is made up, even though all those members taken separately are beautiful. (CF 13.28, p. 344)

This is Augustine's refrain. "We see these things, and they are individually *good* and all together *very good*" (CF 13.32, p. 347). We reach our greater perfection in our relationship with the rest of creation, both in space and in time.

Let your works praise you that we may love you, and let us love you that your works may praise you. For they have a beginning and an end in time, a rising and a setting, growth and decay, form and privation. So they have their succession of morning and evening, in part secretly, in part evident. For they were made of nothing, by you, not of you; not of some matter not made by you or previously in existence, but from matter which was concreated, that is created by you simultaneously with the things made of it, because without any interval of time you gave form to its state that was without form. (CF 13.33, p. 347)

And yet, our temporal perfection is the perfection of the form of the sixth day, which has both morning and evening. And with the evening of the sixth day, "this most beautiful order of things that are very good will finish its course and pass away." So, Augustine prays for "the peace of quiet, the peace of the Sabbath which has no evening" (CF 13.35, p. 349).

The *very good* of the whole is dependent upon the coming to be and passing away of the parts. The challenge of form is thus the mystery of time. The wordless song of creation is given voice only in time. Fiction gives way to philosophy, which in turn gives way to poetry rightly understood, which, in turn, is expressed in praise. *Deus creator omnium*.

"You are the music while the music lasts." The universe is not a stage but a poem. As actors in history we are syllables in a poetic line whose beginning precedes us and whose end is elusive and unfinished. We must speak, in congruity with the words which have come before, but freely, not as their slaves. Each syllable we utter is a choice which forecloses some possibilities even as it opens others. Sometimes our metric foot stumbles; sometimes we have inherited an awkward meter, to which we must lend beauty. But just as if an architect were placed, as a statue, in an angle of a beautiful building, he would only perceive his field of vision and not the edifice as a whole, so too we speak our lines in relative ignorance of the poem's integral beauty. "And in a poem, if syllables should live and perceive only so long as they sound, the harmony and beauty of the connected work would in no way please them. For they could not see or approve the whole, since it would be fashioned and perfected by the very passing away of these singulars" (MS 6.11.30, pp. 355, 356). How do we contribute well to a whole not of our making and whose ultimate shape is known only in intimations?

Augustine's *On Music* is one of his earliest treatises, itself an unfinished part of an unfinished project conceived as a series of works on each of the seven liberal arts. *On Music* is unfinished in that, Augustine tells us that, having written on rhythm, he intended a companion volume on harmony. As for the project on the liberal arts, the task was unfulfilled, save for fragments, only fragments of which survive. Comprising six books, *On Music* is regarded as something of a curiosity in music theory—a late antique critique and extension of earlier musicological treatises. Books 1–5 wrestle with technical matters of poetic rhythm and meter. Book 6 is notable for its more explicitly moral-philosophical content; Augustine himself seems to have presented Book 6 as a stand-alone treatise several decades after the work's completion. Yet, despite Augustine's rhetorical protestations, the work merits consideration as an integral whole, balancing as it does the numerical, social, and cosmological elements of ancient treatises on music. That is, the work itself, a dialogue, enacts the very problem it is trying to address: how do we understand the relation of parts to the whole in time? Additionally, the work undertakes a twofold challenge: how do we understand the relationship between the good, the beautiful, and the true; and how do we teach the relationship to others?

For present purposes we accept that *On Music* stands on its own, without the projected complement of a treatise on harmonics. It is curious, then, that of all the liberal arts, it is music that Augustine chose to complete first. In some sense, an analysis of music provides the fundamental building blocks for understanding the other liberal arts; in another sense, music is the art of arts, the culmination of the other liberal arts in that it includes the study of grammar, rhetoric, logic and mathematics, geometry, and possibly even astronomy. All of these are present, more or less, in Augustine's treatise, but more significantly for our purposes is the work's layered engagement of physics, ethics, and metaphysics—the tripartite account not just of ancient treatises on music but of most works of ancient or late antique philosophy generally. Whereas the modern mind, especially after the introduction of the Bismarckian university, thinks of disciplines as discrete specializations, the ancient mind was curious about the relationships of individual disciplines to the whole. Augustine is also recognizing what Gödel later formally theorized in mathematics—one cannot adequately judge a formal system from within.

Augustine's definition of music comes early in Book 1: "Music is the science of mensurating well (*modulandi*)." Yes, but what does mensuration (*modulatio*) mean? asks an interlocutor, who is identified only as Discipulus (student) in relation to the other speaker, Magister (master). *Modulari*, we are told, comes from *modus* (measure) and the terms of the dialogue are set—what does it mean to measure (or mensurate) and to measure well? (MS 1.2.2, pp. 172, 173).

Even before we have the definition that clarifies the inquiry, the work's dramatic character has given us clues—both substantively and as readers of the work's many poetic examples. "What foot is '*modus*'?" asks Magister. A pyrrhic. "What foot is '*bonus*'?" "The same as '*modus*'?" "So, what is '*bonus*' is also '*modus*'?" No, they are the same in sound (meter) but not in signification. Barely ten lines in, even before a definition of music, the dialogue has opened several questions. First, what is the relationship between *bonus* and *modus*, between the good and the measure? Are *bonus* and *modus* the same? Similar? How are they oriented toward one another? Second, what is the relationship between form (here the metrical foot, the pyrrhic) and content, between sound and signification? Third, how do we understand how things can be at the same time similar and different; or, more precisely, how things can be the same in one category and different in others? To these questions the dialogue will shortly introduce, as it must, the dimension of time. And finally, we must assume that the choice of *bonus* and *modus* is not accidental—the reader is placed on notice to observe not just the sound of the examples but the signification.

From the very start, then, even the most technical discussions of ancient meter are framed by ethical and metaphysical concerns. While Book 6 may well stand on its own, *On Music* as a whole, like *On the Trinity*, is a pedagogical journey, a training of the mind and soul, a process of purification, a cleansing of false conceptions so that true conceptions may emerge (MS 6.1.1, pp. 324, 325).

The account here will include matters of technical theory only insofar as they are immediately relevant to the questions at hand. The dialogue's musical-theoretical dimensions are well treated elsewhere; what concerns us is the relationship between Augustine's treatment of rhythm and his moral-aesthetic theory, which has been largely neglected.

What does it mean to say that music is a science? There are those who know the theory but cannot perform well; others perform but are not in possession of the theoretical knowledge. And to what extent is music a matter of physical practice and memory? Even animals make beautiful sounds, and yet they do so (says the argument in the dialogue) out of sense memory and imitation, not because they possess the theoretical knowledge. Similarly, actors and singers may perform by habit, without the rational knowledge of their art. Moreover, actors and singers (and, in the background, we are to understand orators or rhetoricians as well) perform for pay and celebrity, not for the sake of their art. In the case of birds, for example, music is not a rational expression; in the case of actors, the expression may be rational but it is a means to another end and not an end in itself.

The discussion comes to rest on the conclusion that music, properly speaking, is a practice of reason for its own sake, a mensurating well which is intrinsically good, and not pursued for outside advantage. Whether in music or in dance—the argument is framed with respect to a certain skill in moving—mensuration is applied "to that movement which is free, that is, desired for itself and charms through itself alone." And so Magister and Discipulus conclude: "The science of mensurating is the science of moving well, in such a way that the movement is desired for itself" (MS 1.2.3, p. 175). The dialogue thus affirms music's status as a liberal, that is, free and freeing, rather than a servile art.

The science of movement gives way in the dialogue to the science of numbers, which is at once mathematical and mystical. Because they are discussing "numerically ordered movements,"

Magister and Discipulus elect to "consider numbers themselves," exploring the "fixed laws numbers make manifest" (MS 1.11.19, p. 194). The science of the mensuration of movement is dependent upon the law of numbers. The exploration of the laws of numbers, however, resolves very quickly into the exploration of the relationship among numbers, which is to say, the study of ratios and proportions. This makes sense, for mensurating must take place in reference to a standard, or at least in reference to something else. For the time being, Magister and Discipulus are interested only in the latter, discerning the ways in which ordered patterns make "a one from many," creating (or revealing) a harmony and unity that is worthy of admiration and love (MS 1.12.22, pp. 198, 199). Symmetry and sequence effect a loveable unity through proportion (or, in Greek, *analogia*), which is the growth, as it were, of the numbers one and two: "the beginnings and seeds, as it were, of numbers" (MS 1.12.25, p. 202). It is only through proportion that we begin to apprehend individuals in relation to the whole.

The science of numbers and the science of proportion are different, and the difference lies at the heart of Augustine's musical project. In Book 2, the course of the dialogue explicitly takes on the authority of the grammarians, for whom number, not proportion, is pre-eminent. Grammar "prefers the conservation of historical precedent"; the grammarian is "the guardian of history" who lays down the laws of rhythm as an incontrovertible authority. The grammarian is, so to speak, the embodiment of positive law understood as fidelity to the past alone, not as the possibility of creative freedom in the future.

In contrast, the "reason of music," which is to say, proportion, takes its bearings from authority or custom, but considers a syllable "according to the rationale of its measure." That is, it proceeds according to the judgment of nature, not according to a slavish notion of the past. Grammar, in its embrace of rhythm, maintains absolute numerical equality. Music, in Augustine's conception, gives primacy to meter and rhythm, and so maintains proportional equality among syllables which are unlike. There are at least three issues at hand.

First, which is superior, the authority of history or the reason of nature? Second, is unity found in identity of substance or equality of form? Third, what are the possibilities of innovation, and on what basis may innovation occur? That is, on what basis are freedom and creativity possible?

The dialogue places the judgment of reasoned sense above the authority of the grammarians. Following the grammatical rules slavishly can cause offense to the ear; so too can breaking the rules yield a pleasant sound. In the "reason of music," the rationale of measure, relations of proportion determine what is beautiful, not the weight of history, authority, and tradition. To discern what syllable is permitted where requires the capacity to discriminate "between what the sense of hearing demands and what authority demands" (MS 2.2.2, p. 208). In departing from authority, however, not just any combination of syllables will do. "For when I see feet of all sorts thrown together, many and without end, I shall not call them a verse." Ratio, then, stands between authority and randomness. A verse "is generated by ratio" (MS 2.7.14, pp. 221, 222).

Rhythm has a regularity grounded in numerical equality. The beat is even, equal, and with no exceptions. Rhythm is, we might say, mechanical in its regularity. The primacy of rhythm, then, subordinates difference to numerical regularity. Equality of rhythm is identity or sameness. Meter subordinated to rhythm admits little if any freedom. By contrast, rhythm subordinated to meter allows difference to flourish without abandoning order. Basing the poetic foot on meter rather than rhythm allows for a freer range of ordered combinations.

Two different notions of equality are operative. Numerical equality prioritizes identity of substance, whereas proportional equality allows inequality or difference of substance within equality of form. Despite the grammarians' rules, any foot (the dialogue identifies 28 different feet) may be combined with any other "provided an equality [of form] is preserved. For what can give the ear more pleasure than being both delighted by variety and uncheated of equality?" (MS 2.10.16, pp. 224, 225). Proportional equality prompts consideration of "the interrelation of the parts within the other feet" (MS 2.10.18, p. 226).

To prove the point, Magister composes a short verse on the spot, finding in the combined syllables "a single equality and a multiform difference" (MS 2.13.24, p. 233). The verse is pleasing, but breaks the rules. After a relentless technical exploration of the possible combination of metric feet, Magister suggests they "breathe a little" and return to the spontaneous verse:

> Volo tandem tibi parcas, labor est in chartis,
> Et apertum ire per auras animum permittas.
> Placet hoc nam sapientur, remitter interdum
> Aciem rebus agendis decenter intentam.

"And now I want you to spare yourself (there is drudgery in letters), and to let your mind run free to the winds. For this is a judicious pleasure, to relax at times your attention when it has been properly trained to business" (MS 2.14.26, p. 236). The drama of the dialogue is itself enacting the sound and rest of poetry, and of learning itself. Exertion must be punctuated with rest, just as silence becomes an important element, giving form to syllables by marking their beginning and ending, as well as contributing to the meter of versification, as the dialogue subsequently stresses.

The discussion next turns to the relationship between rhythm, meter, and verse, with an emphasis on meter. The structure recalls Augustine's later triad: number, measure, and weight. Not all rhythm is meter and not all meter is verse. The dialogue speaks explicitly and repeated about the laws of versification, emphasizing that the disciple has knowledge of rational principles—by ear, as it were—without the need of specialized grammatical terminology. But reason also prefers "that which is prior in the order of feet." There is freedom in Augustine's conception of verse composition, but that freedom is bounded jointly by the laws of versification (understood according to reason and taste, not blind obedience to authority) and by what has come before (that is, so to speak, history). What is prior in the order of feet—the meter that has come before—requires a response if the verse is to be coherent. Rather than being determinative, the prior feet of a verse still admit "a very great number of choices" allowing for remaining feet "lawfully mixed in" (MS 3.4.9, p. 246). The poet responds both to nature and to history.

Both reason and the laws of versification recognize that silence too has a time value. In measuring a verse, what appears to be a defect is often a failure to account for a rest (*silentium*) which itself adds length to the metric foot: an empty time. How then do we think of a rest as part of a verse, defined as "two members joined and measured in fixed ratio"? (MS 3.4.9, p. 246). That is, how do we think about the ratio of silence? The law and ratio of meter itself can force a silence, a breath, a pause, a temporary Sabbath, as it were, just as the dialogue took a pause after considerable intellectual exertion. The sound of silence (what the Japanese call *ma*—the slight pause or gap between two musical notes) is a part of meter.

Book 4 is a virtuosic tour of metrical combinations, extraordinary for its technical depth and range. What is of interest here is the substance of the poetic examples given (MS 4.3.4-4.6.7, pp. 264–70). The first, illustrating pyrrhics:

Quid est homo
Qui amat hominem,
Si amat in eo
Fragile quod est?

"What is man? What does a man love if he loves that which perishes?"

A series of similar pyrrhics follows, illustrating different combinations often using a metric rest, culminating in "one remaining meter of this kind with a more joyful sentence":

Solida bona bonus amat, et ea quit amat, habet.
Itaque nec eget amor, et ea bona Deus est.

"The good man loves the lasting good, and he has that which he loves. Therefore, he is not in need if he loves the good that is God."

The technical arc of the conversation is the illustration of fourteen different kinds of pyrrhic combinations, but the moral content of the examples is unavoidable. What will a man be who loves that which is fragile or fleeting? Loving that which is good is to love that which endures or is solid, which is to say, God.

Fourteen examples of iambic follow, beginning:

Bonus vir
Beatus
Malus miser,
Sibi est malum.

"The good man is happy, the bad man is unhappy, and it is an evil to him."
And ending with:

Beatus est videns Deum, nihil boni amplius volet,
Malus foris bonum requirit, hinc eget miser bono.

"Happy is the one who sees God, for he shall not desire a fuller good. The bad man seeks for a door to the good, and so lacks the good."
The fourteenth example of trochee:

Veritate facta cuncta sunt, et ordinate cuncta,
Veritas manens novat, moventur ut noventur ista.

"Deeds are joined together and ordered in truth. Truth persisting makes things new, and is moved so that it may make things new."
The fourteenth spondee:

Solus liber iure ac non falso securam vitam vivit,
Qui erroris vinclum tetrum ac funestum prudens iam devicit.

"He alone is free who lives by what is right and not false, and so lives life well. He who is tied to error is foul and destructive, rapidly subduing the foresight of prudence."
The good man is happy in the vision of God. Truth is bound to what is ordinate, and freedom loves that which is just and true. To read each sequence of fourteen examples in order is to watch not only the metric variations unfold, but to see the unfolding of a compact moral teaching. The law and ratio of meter give form to the combination of syllables, which in turn give form to the sounds we hear and therefore the thoughts we form. In his own way, Augustine has echoed Plato's exile of the poets from the city, and then effected their readmission, turning poetry from immoral to moral uses.

Book 4 concludes with a recognition that, thanks to the judicious use of the rest (*silentium*), the number of possible metric variations is almost infinite: "the number is so great its name perhaps is not at hand" (MS 4.17.37, p. 296). Yet each is measured, each lawful in its formal qualities. The question is whether these formal variations are oriented to good or evil, to happiness or misery, to truth or falsehood, to freedom or servitude.

Book 5 takes up the burden of the content of verse indirectly in its consideration of verse as such. Again, the examples are telling. The first: *Roma, Roma, cerne quanta sit eum benignitas*. But the bulk of the discussion is perhaps "the most famous of all" heroic verses: *Arma virumque cano, Troiae qui primus ab oris*. The metrical example illustrates, among other things, that that which is beautiful defies categorization, even as the regularities of meter and verse give rise to the beautiful (MS 5.10.21, p. 315).

But if we accept the parallel of number, measure, and weight with rhythm, meter, and verse, then verse carries the weight of love. That is, the subject matter of the verse, whether epic or lyric, forms and is formed by our love. Here, verse—like the Roman mind—is dominated by Rome, the god's favor, of arms—the song is the narrative of republic and empire.

Both formally and in content, Augustine in *On Music* is setting the stage for understanding how the narrative journeys are framed, and how those frames are filled with content. And he is preparing to use the order of rhythm, meter, and verse to shift the epic story from that of the earthly city of Rome—the song of arms and war—to that of the pilgrim seeking divine rest—the song of creation. Let us turn, he says at the conclusion of Book 5, "with as much wisdom as we can from these sensible traces of music, all dealing with that part of it in the numbers of the times to the real places where it is free of all body" (MS 5.13.28, p. 323).

The regularities of metrical change in time lead to a shift "from the fleshly senses and letters" to "the love of unchangeable truth." The passage is not an easy one, says Magister, and the time spent "dwelling with grammatical and poetical minds" in Books 1–5 was itself a pilgrimage with temporary company, "through necessity of wayfaring." The books were of necessity technical and for specialized minds, particularly those who, "given up to secular letters, are involved in great errors and waste their natural good qualities in vanities, not knowing what their charm is." Books 1–5 then have a twofold pedagogy: the conversion of grammarians from the poetry of deception to the music of the word, and the intellectual preparation of the mind to behold the beauty of the music of the word beyond sound (MS 6.1.1, pp. 324, 325).

To pass from corporeal to incorporeal things, Magister proposes this verse: *Deus creator omnium*. The relation between *bonus* and *modus* which launches the dialogue has been recast from singing of arms and men to the epic poem of God's creative act—from Vergil's narrative of Aeneas to Genesis itself. The verse which defines the whole is no longer the tragic epic of earthly political life but the metaphysics of created nature.

What are the ears by which we hear and judge what is beautiful, aesthetically and morally? What is experienced as harmonious is recognized as such because we have within us the soundless numbers and ratios of the song of creation. Sound does not bring its harmony to us, but is received by us and approved or rejected according to its coincidence with the harmony within us, "like a trace imprinted in water, not found before your pressing a body into it, and not remaining when you have taken it away" (MS 6.2.3, pp. 326–28).

Hearing and evaluating sound involved, for Augustine, five kinds of numbers: the sound, the judgment of sense, the judgment of mind, the memory, and natural judgment.

> For it is one thing to sound and this is attributed to a body; another to hear, and in the body the soul is passive to this from sounds; another to produce numbers either more slow or less so; another to remember them; and another, by accepting or rejecting, to give sentence on them all as if by some natural right (*quasi quodam naturali iure ferre sententiam*). (MS 6.4.5, pp. 329, 330)

The fifth kind of number Augustine terms judicial numbers—the numbers by which we judge—and the explicitly judicial language is striking. And just as Augustine speaks of the laws of rhythm, meter, and verse, it is interesting to reflect on the intersection (in English and French at least) of speaking a sentence and giving a sentence ("sentencing" a person in punishment for a crime), where both uses refer to some sense of natural right (*ius*) or justice (*iustitia*).

The first four kinds of number are temporal; they pass in and out of sound, sense, mind, and memory. The judicial numbers, however, endure in our nature because they take their form from God. Like the ratio of numbers themselves, which have a beginning, middle, and end, the soul occupies a middle between the sense and the intellect. The body receives impressions through the sense which it judges according to the numbers imprinted on it by God. The judicial numbers receive sense data and judge it according to their harmony with the internal form. Properly, the soul shapes the sense impressions to a more beautiful form, hearing the beauty that is there but recognizing its echoes of a more permanent beauty. Improperly, the soul is shaped by the lesser beauties of sense perception, which obscure the eternal harmonies (MS 6.4.7-6.5.12, pp. 332–37).

The soul itself is a kind of verse, so to speak, striving to match in some harmonious way the sense perceptions from below, as it were, which nonetheless have their own beauty, with the reasons from above, the source of beauty. The greater the "unity of health" of the soul, which acts quietly to forge "some domestic pact" between sense and reason, the more it shapes its passions rather than being shaped by them. This unity of health hinges on the orientation of our attention. The movement of the soul, like the movement of syllables in time, is unquiet if formed by the irregular meter of bodily passions, like vibrations disrupting the smooth spinning of a long-playing record. But when the soul comes to rest through attention to the divine, it "enjoys an interior freedom of peace signified by the Sabbath. So he knows God alone is his Lord, and He is served with the greatest freedom" (MS 6.5.14, pp. 338, 339). A truly free movement is directed to its own beauty (MS 6.10.25, p. 351). Here the numbers speak with a kind of silence reflecting a freedom from signification, an immediacy beyond representation—virtuosic action so internalized as to be spontaneous, rather than the calculated response to a specific set of rules. We play the moral life by ear. To know the form is to love beyond the rule.

And so we have the reprieve of a theme introduced in Book 1—is music a science of mensuration or a habit? To what extent is virtuosic action the product of reason or of habit and imitation? One difficulty in answering the question comes from a limitation to the judicial numbers which inhere in human nature. By virtue of our temporality, our mortality, we are unable to judge longer intervals—we can only view a fragmentary slice of the poem of the universe.

> [T]o each living thing in its proper kind and in its proportion with the universe is given a sense of places and times, so that even as its body is so much in proportion to the body of the universe whose part it is, and its age so much in proportion to

the age of the universe whose part it is, so its sensing complies with the action it pursues in proportion to the movement of the universe whose part it is. (MS 6.7.19, pp. 343, 344)

We are limited in time, by time. As such, our natures are necessarily shaped by our times, for "it is not for nothing custom is called a sort of second and fitted-on nature. But we see new senses in the judging of this kind of corporeal things, built by custom, by another custom disappear" (MS 6.7.19, p. 344). Our judicial numbers, while participating in the eternal, are nonetheless partial with respect to eternity. Each generation must judge for itself in terms appropriate to the age; the recitation of an ancient poem simply will not do.

Our relation to other created beings is thus itself dominated by our relation to time itself. Just as in the consideration of meter, the consideration of being in time entails the primacy of relations over substance. How do we order things in time so as to achieve equality of relations? And how do we form the attention so that, as so often happens, Augustine says, "being occupied with another thought, we do not in conversation seem to have heard even ourselves"? (MS 6.8.21, pp. 345, 346). That is, how do the motions of our souls attend to what is needed by the times and places in which we live?

The promise of the music of the word culminates in the four classical virtues infused with desire augmented to *caritas*. We return to Augustine's questions from Book 3 of *Confessions*, What do we love when we love beauty? Here the question is transposed to musical terms. "'What is it we love in sensible harmony?' 'Nothing but a sort of equality and equally measured intervals.'" Equally measured intervals includes silences, rests, "in the spread of time." The equality also reinforces the sense of differences in substance but equality of relations, putting the emphasis on relations. Mechanical relations consider only the substance as a product of efficient causality; musical relations expand to attend to relations in terms of formal causality—in poetry, the ear "delights in unequals as equals," preserving both the order of the whole and the integrity of the past (MS 6.10.28, p. 354).

This order of the whole in harmony with the integrity of the past is what delights us, what prompts us to adhere to it, to love it. "For delight is a kind of weight in the soul. Therefore, delight orders the soul. 'For where your treasure is, there will your heart be also.'

Where delight, there the treasure; where the heart, there happiness or misery" (MS 6.11.29, p. 355).

Delight is shaped by our understanding of the poem of which we conceive ourselves a part: the epic which trumpets *arma virumque* or that which hymns *Deus creator omnium*. The things of time "are beautiful in their kind and order" but they are nonetheless intimations of eternity in obedience to "the laws of equality, unity, and order." But terrestrial and celestial things "and their time circuits join together in harmonious succession for a poem of the universe" (MS 6.11.29, p. 355).

This cycle, the *periodos* in poetic terms, is not the cycle of history as understood by Polybius, or even the cycle of regimes of Plato and Aristotle. This cycle (*circuitum*) as a form of verse is a ratio "used for the return to the beginning [and] is also used for passing to another such combination" (MS 4.17.35, p. 295). The recursion of pattern is not a repetition of substance but a cycle of form which preserves the absolute uniqueness of every creature in time and space while admitting the potential for proportional equality, though not numerical identity. Two meters of verses can have the same patterns while being otherwise radically different in content. We are syllables or feet in the poem of time, sometimes re-enacting pre-existing patterns, sometimes creating new measures from old feet. Our task is to perceive, as best we can, the poem of the whole of which we are only a part.

And we must perceive the poem of the whole after "losing the whole" through sin (MS 6.11.30, p. 356). That is to say, we make our contribution to the poem of the universe in a condition of ignorance (of the whole) and infirmity (in willing the private rather than the whole) which separates us from the judicial numbers "pre-eminent by virtue of the beauty of ratio" (MS 6.11.31, p. 356).

The conversation of Book 6 suggests that what we have learned about the motion of sounds can also be applied to the soundless "spiritual motions"; these, "in so far as they are simpler ... demand few words, and the greatest possible serenity of mind" (MS 6.12.34, p. 358). Here the beauty of form and substance becomes most acute. That which we direct the mind to most, that for which we have the greatest care, is that which we love the most. And since "we can only love beautiful things," we must consider their relative beauty. The things of lesser beauty "please by number," whereas the equality of ratio or proportion, that is measure, characterizes the objects of greater or higher or nobler beauty.

Just as we delight "in light itself holding the origin of all colors," we delight in the equality in unity of all things, according to their proper nature. "When, then, we seek things suitable for the way of our nature and reject things unsuitable we yet know are suitable to other living things, aren't we here, too, rejoicing in some law of equality when we recognize equals allotted in more subtle ways?" (MS 6.13.38, p. 363). Proportional equality requires attention not only to the relations among creatures, but with respect to a creature's place in the order of nature.

Yet, numerical beauty interferes with our apprehension of proportional beauty, turning the soul away from eternal things, making it restless with the beauty of bodies, distracting it with the phantasms of memory, and distorting truth itself with vain intellectual curiosity. Rather than being fully itself in relation to the whole, the soul prefers to imitate God perversely, rejecting the proportional equality appropriate to creatures and substituting the lust for domination.

> But that appetite of the soul is to have under it other souls; not of beasts as conceded by divine law, but rational ones, that is, your neighbors, fellows and companions under the same law. But the proud soul desires to operate on them, and as much as every soul is better than every body, just so much does the action on them seem more excellent than on bodies. But God alone can operate on rational souls, not through a body, but through Himself. But such is the state of sin that souls are allowed to act upon souls moving them by signifying by one or the other body, or by natural signs as look or nod, or by conventional signs as words. For they act with signs by commanding or persuading, and if there is any other way besides command and persuasion, souls act with or upon other souls. But by rights it has come about those souls wishing to be over others command their own parts and bodies with difficulty and pain, in part being foolish in themselves, in part, oppressed by mortal members. And so with these numbers and motions souls set upon souls by, with the desire of honor and praise they are turned away from the sight of that pure and entire truth. For God alone honors the soul making it blessed in secret when it lives justly and piously before Him. (MS 6.13.41, p. 365)

In our desire to operate on rational souls in imitation of God, we step outside the equality of the verse that is proper to us; in desiring to be like God we disrupt the beauty of the poem of the universe, doing injustice to the whole and injuring the peace within ourselves.

We are, then, looking for equality, for likeness, for beauty in all the wrong places and desire that which is barely a shadow or trace of the divine light, causing the soul to "sink from the truest height of equality ... and build up earthy machines in its own ruins" (MS 6.14.44, p. 367). By contrast, scripture and the proper understanding of the five numbers point to the twofold commandment to love God and neighbor. "If, then, we refer all those motions and numbers of human action to this end, we shall certainly be cleansed. Isn't it so?" asks Magister. "It certainly is," replies Discipulus, "but how short this is to learn, and how hard and arduous to do" (MS 6.14.43, p. 366, 367).

In loving lower beauties, the soul loses not only equality, but its own order as well. Its relationship to others and to itself is no longer in equilibrium. "For it is one thing to keep order and another to be kept by order. That soul keeps order that, with its whole self, loves Him above itself, that is, God and fellow souls as itself" (MS 6.14.46, p. 368). But even those souls in the greatest disequilibrium understand and seek the bond of order insofar as it recognizes even the slightest traces of beauty.

So it is that the experience of poetry, the music of the word, the recognition of proportion and ratio in sound and silence, in presence and absence, yield the four classical virtues. For moderating the bodily passions is temperance; standing firm in pursuit of eternal joy in the face of temporal loss is fortitude; the soul ordering itself to serve God and desiring "to be co-equal to only the purest souls and to have dominion only over animal and corporeal nature" is justice; and prudence is "the virtue the soul knows its proper station by, its ascent to it being through temperance, that is, conversion of love to God called charity, and aversion from this world attended by fortitude and justice" (MS 6.15.50–51, pp. 371, 372).

Music entails each of the virtues individually and culminates in the virtues collectively, unified in and by love. Music fixes our love in God, reforming the soul which has lapsed "by pride into certain actions of its own power," and which, "neglecting universal law, has fallen into doing certain private things to itself" (MS 6.16.53, p. 374). So it is that "even the sinful and miserable soul may be moved by numbers," and when those numbers inhere in lesser loves, they nonetheless "can't lack beauty entirely." Being "beautiful in equality and likeness, and bound by order," number reminds us of the unity from which we were created, and of the proper order in place or time or weight. In music, our soul utters the confession that "all things whatever and of any size are made from one beginning through a form equal to it and like to the riches of His goodness, by which they are joined together in charity as one and one gift from one" (MS 6.17.56, p. 375).

The plurality of forms within God who speaks creation guarantees the proportional equality and individuality of each creature in time, while also allowing for the unity of created diversity. Augustine's formulation resists pantheism and borders on panentheism, through the likeness of similitude of the parts and the whole, just as an artisan can fashion individual forms in wood in reference to the "numbers of his art" (MS 6.17.57, p. 376). This is true, says Augustine, not only in space but also in the circle or period of time. The same poem read aloud is both the same and different each time it is spoken.

Each poem spoken is a whispered echo of the divine poem of the universe. And the more beautiful the poem, the more the divine beauty shines through. As the soul is moved from beauty to love and worship, the air reverberates with the sounds of *Deus creator omnium*, which creates even as we co-create by lending our own feet to the meter of time.

On Music, especially Books 1–5, is a purification of the soul by reasoning, intended for the philosophical few. And in this, Augustine develops a sophisticated new grammar of the soul and its relation to creation. But while *On Music* is directed toward the few, poetry charms all to the beauty, proportion, and collective virtue of the whole.

Finally, we might say that the hierarchy of rhythm (that is to say, number) may be expressed in the proportional co-equality of meter. The order of verse, then, not only reconciles the plurality and unity of individual creatures in time and space, but also synthesizes that natural hierarchy of numbers with the proportional equality of forms.

Placing our feet in the poetry of creation forges a frame of judgment and opens a different window neglected in the Enlightenment. The tempering of reason by beauty retains the rationality of number and meter, but situates them, softened, in the dappled beauty of verse. That is, verse places reason in the service of judgment, the sense of what is fitting. Obedience to the law, then, is neither the slavish service to reason nor the immoral expression of will detached from reason. Rather, it is situated in circumstances bound by time and place, yet free in creative response; improvisational, not imitative, the lapping beat of the call and response of psalter and spiritual song. Freedom is put in service of love. "The law of liberty is the law of love."

In being bound by the beauty of the law, we respond not to its rigidity, but to the creative possibilities it permits. Love of the whole is our reference point, a love which dispels the darkness of the shadowed corners of the private. Reason is resolved into understanding; what is fitting is not what is rational but what is wise.

7

The Law of Liberty and the Law of Love

The law is a gesture of love's architecture, which says everything. Logic, the Logos, took the form of love, not to remove the teeth from law but to guard against the dangerous moods of reason. The language of love has given way to the logic of rights; freedom has driven duty from the field of action. Can we be bound by the beauty of the law which expresses itself in the music of the word? Liberty and love are improvisations bound by the beauty of the law. Our Augustinian pilgrimage is an unrehearsed spiritual adventure, a sallying forth into the punctuations of sacred time and space as things unfold in their coming to be and passing away. Where are we—individually and collectively—in our journey of learning to live according to our higher justice, our greater perfection? Is it possible to transpose Augustine's frameworks into our own? What shoots of his thinking can we graft upon the trunks of our own, or vice versa, what grafts of our thinking may bear better fruit for being placed in Augustinian soil? Can the beauty of the law cascading from creation and toward our greatest potential be sufficient to bind us together not just in utility but in justice and in love?

For Augustine, creation aims for the community of the whole, partly because, as social beings, we find our fullness in being a part of a whole; and partly because we complement the whole by bringing our specific character to the whole. This is an Aristotelian and Ciceronian sociability of the whole—human beings are, by nature, social animals who are both physically and morally sustained in community. But it also has echoes of John Stuart Mill, who in *On Liberty* accentuates the importance of the eccentric character, the social outlier, who brings an almost genetic social diversity which nourishes and revitalizes the social body in conditions of freedom.

The tension between public and private, between communal and individual, is thus at its best a creative one.

The creative natural and historical social tensions arise most fully in conditions characterized by the liberties and limitations which obtain in non-oppressive hierarchical relationships. The story of modern freedom is the liberation from oppressive hierarchical relationships, to the extent that we have forgotten even the possibility of non-oppressive hierarchical relationships. More acutely, we have come to see all hierarchical relationships as necessarily oppressive, and for good reasons—offices are occupied by human beings struggling with pride and fear. Moreover, we have come to see the holding of an office as a locus of power rather than a temporary role of duties of service and responsibility.

Augustine derives his conception of what is right from the structure of duties. By contrast, Thomas Hobbes, in his *On the Citizen*, begins with a discussion of rights, and only later takes up a discussion of duties. What I claim on others precedes what others owe to me, or what I owe to others. Put slightly differently, in a framework that begins with rights, the first thing I owe another is forbearance—the restraint not to impinge upon another's rights. The language of rights is the language of assertion, of claim upon another. Rights must be respected, at a minimum, and at a maximum they impose a duty on others. If I have a right to life, there must be some guarantee of protection from others who seek to take away my life. Similarly, if I have a right to (say) education, then there is a duty on another to satisfy that claim.

The grammar of rights, then, participates in the structure of efficient causality. In asserting rights, either theoretically or practically, we attempt to shape the matter of social relationships. But to what end? Is the language of rights enough to bind a people together? Rights are the province of individuals; even if they are guaranteed by a society, are rights alone sufficient ligaments for community?

For Hobbes, the first law of nature is self-preservation. In this sense, law is used in the same sense of the law of gravity. It is a motive force, an efficient cause. But the law of nature is also a principle of rational action—I should act to preserve my lift because it is reasonable to do so. Correspondingly, Hobbes says, because I want to preserve myself, it is natural, instinctively and rationally, to seek peace.

In Hobbes's construction, the language of rights has its origin in the language of law understood as a dictate of reason, a command of reason. Natural law gives way to natural right which in turn yields positive law, where positive law is the dictate of an agreed-upon authority. Reason is mediated through will.

Hobbes, of course, is keen to show that this structure of right and law is not inconsistent with the witness of Christian scripture; nevertheless, the foundation of his system of rights and laws is divorced from both a theology of creation and the framework of Aristotelian causality. The order of nature, for Hobbes, is the order of matter; causality is mechanistic, including human psychology, which he sees in terms of the mechanisms of sense perception. The frontispiece of *Leviathan* makes the framework clear through omission: "Of the Matter, Cause, and Form of the Commonwealth." The final cause is formally and intentionally unarticulated.

Of course, the end toward which Hobbes's commonwealth is directed is peace, but this peace is understood as the absence of the conflict of wills in a system of mechanistic, efficient causality. Rights and laws are shaped in the absence of a conception of the beauty of creation directed toward the unfolding of the soul understood in terms of formal and final causality.

Hobbes is an exemplary pivot point in our thinking about the relationship between law and right. He is much more ancient and medieval than conventional contract theorists tend to appreciate. His formal structure is, in large measure, quite Augustinian. The earthly city aims at an earthly peace, which is itself a good, both *in se* and as the precondition for other earthly goods. Law is a function of reason, not of will.

For understandable reasons, both theoretical and practical, Hobbes has removed the Augustinian logic from the framework of creation and final causality. Peace as the cessation of conflicting wills is not the realization of the Sabbath rest. Similarly, reason as divorced from the structure of creation places law in the hands of human beings alone. Without authority there is no law, says Hobbes, and without law there is no justice, no mine and thine. Justice is derived from the power to keep men in awe. Right shapes positive law which in turn shapes justice. There is, for Hobbes, no natural justice; there is nothing properly due to another human being apart from obedience to the sovereign's rational decree, which takes as its reckoning point the maintenance of peace.

Significantly, both Hobbes and Augustine see law as a command of reason. For Augustine, as we have seen, reason is embedded in a framework of created nature, which, philosophically, Hobbes does not share. Perhaps beginning with Rousseau, a shared reason (understood as a binding command) gives way to a general will—politics ceases to be obedience to the command of reason in favor of the assertion of the will.

There is one further complication. When translating his own *On the Citizen* from Latin to English, Hobbes renders the Latin *iustitia* as "righteousness." On the one hand, this translation is quite straightforward: the Latin *ius* means "right." On the other hand, there is a double confusion. First, what is the relationship between right and law, between *ius* and *lex*? Second, what is the relationship between what is just and what is righteous or holy?

If Hobbes occupies a kind of pivot in our thinking about law and right, preserving an Augustinian logic in a modern, mechanistic-materialist framework, later contract theory keeps a Hobbesian logic but removes it from the frame of reason altogether.

This account of Hobbes, more exemplary than historical, lays bare the complexity of the conceptual mosaic of the source and directionality of law. The late modern conception of law begins with rights and orients law through the will (of the people or of a person). Augustine's conception of right is derived from law understood as a command of reason embedded in the scale of natural value. The rights-based system is centripetal and potentially expansive; the law-based system is centrifugal and has the tendency to collapse upon human freedom. Hobbes himself described this as the tension between too much liberty on the one hand and too much authority on the other. I have just used a Newtonian image of circular motion to illustrate the inherent directionality of systems of law and right. Conceiving of rights primarily in terms of efficient causality bends toward the assertion of self toward freedom understood as autonomy *(autonomia)*—literally being a law unto oneself. Law as a formal cause bends toward the limitation of self in service to an end which is outside oneself.

Efficient cause, formal cause. Right, law. Freedom, authority. Will, reason. Justice, holiness-as-righteousness. These are not binaries but dynamic tensions which, like any tension, pull toward one polarity or the other. What harmony is best able to form a people, to bind a people together?

The modern notion of rights entails a particular vision of freedom, well characterized by Benjamin Constant. In his speech "The Liberty of the Ancients Compared with That of the Moderns," Constant characterized ancient liberty as the limitation of the private sphere for liberty in the public sphere. This is what Isaiah Berlin would later call positive liberty—*freedom for*, or realized in, the community. Modern freedom, for Constant, prizes the liberty of the private, the limitation of the community in favor of individual freedom. This Berlin called negative liberty—*freedom from* interference by the community. One might say that ancient freedom recognized a formal and final cause, while modern freedom puts its weight on material and efficient causality. Our challenge, according to Constant, is to realize the best of both kinds of liberty while minimizing the corporatist and individualist dangers of each, respectively. In effect, Constant has renewed the Ciceronian-Augustinian problematic—how to align the private and the public. Civic republicanism emphasizes public duties.

If Constant looked to the Greeks in thinking about the character of modern freedom, Hannah Arendt looked to the Romans for thinking about authority. Moderns, she contends in her essay "What Is Authority?" have forgotten what authoritative relationships might be. She distinguishes between authority and force; the former is voluntary (I obey freely because I respect the authority of the person who commands), while the latter is involuntary (I obey because the person who commands can bring physical coercion to bear). For Arendt, the most familiar modern example of authority is the coach—we do what the coach commands because we have voluntarily submitted to his or her authority, defer to his judgment and trust that she has our best interest (individually and as a team) at heart. There is freedom within constraint, there is a challenge to growth and a vision of excellence. In such a hierarchical, authoritative relationship it makes no sense for me to think of being liberated from an oppressive coach, except insofar as I cease to experience the relationship as beneficial and withhold my obedience—at which point the relationship is no longer authoritative.

For Augustine, the field of authority extended well beyond that of a coach, encompassing both natural and customary social relationships: parent-child; paterfamilias-household; consul-populi (and all the attendant political relationships of the Roman Republic); priest-devotee; patron-client. Arendt observes that these relationships were intensely personal—based on personal knowledge and interaction. While systemic, these relationship were personal, not bureaucratic. A bureaucrat has power; a person exercising a duty has, as we say, "moral authority" which ushers from both the office or role and the individual character of the person in authority. The possibilities of abuse are, of course, considerable in settings where the dominant party disregards Cicero's counsel and acts from pride and power rather than a sense of duty and justice, or if the sense of duty and justice is skewed.

Tradition too, for Arendt, has the weight of authority—we obey traditions voluntarily if indeed they are authoritative partly because of habit, to be sure, but also because we have an understanding of how a custom nourishes and sustains both the individual and the whole of social life. A dead tradition ceases to be authoritative—we speak of the force of custom—but a living tradition adapts and changes with innovation carried out within recognizable limits, just as in styles of painting or genres of music.

Modern social and political organization, in Arendt's view, has abandoned this understanding of the personal and traditional authority. Among the three structures of command and obedience— authority, persuasion, and force—only authority is voluntary: persuasion and force, for Arendt, are ultimately coercive. So it is that totalitarian regimes rule by persuasion (propaganda and psychological fear) and physical force (or its threat). Paradoxically, even non-totalitarian systems tend toward the erosion of freedom to the extent that they cease to be characterized by relationships of authority. Relationships, especially including bureaucratic relationships, limit the freedom and damage the dignity of both parties in a non-authoritative hierarchical relationship.

Relationships of force, as distinct from authority, limit the discretion of the power-holding person. An official who possesses authority exercises judgment within a range of possible authorized actions. A bureaucrat who has power enforces a policy without the latitude for discretion; he is a cog in an impersonal machine, the transmitter of a power that is not his, a conduit of efficient causality in which he and the object of his force are both unfree. That is, relationships of bureaucratic power dehumanize both she who commands and he who obeys—both are no longer persons exercising reach but are appendages to an impersonal machine.

Arendt's argument, then, is that only authoritative relationships of voluntary command and obedience can counteract the texture of the modern technical bureaucratic state, whether it is explicitly or implicitly totalitarian. The image she gives of authority is that of a many-layered pyramid—authority may be derived from the individual or legislative body at the top, but cascades down widely through many individuals and many layers, each issuing commands with discretion, exercising the duties of service appropriate to their office, and each obeying voluntarily because they conceive of the good of the whole and themselves. By contrast, Arendt sees the relationships of power in terms of an onion, where all power radiates from a single center, organically and inexorably. A defect in any part is necessarily a defect in the whole, for the part no longer has its independence—it is absorbed into the whole. By contrast still, the individual authority within the pyramid of authority is kept in balance by the other individuals in the whole, for by definition the authoritative relationships contain a range of freedom within limits and so have a flexible tension, a range of tolerance of permitted movement.

For Arendt, when authoritative relationships recede or are dissolved, what is left is the despotism of one at the top of the pyramid and the slavish equality of all at the bottom, with no intermediary authority. In this, she implicitly echoes Tocqueville's analysis of the tendency of democracies toward despotism, where the intermediate authorities of federated government and of voluntary associations no longer moderate the exercise of power. Arendt nods to the Catholic (carrying on the Roman tradition) of subsidiarity—effectively a pyramid of authority in which authority is ideally located at the level closest to those affected by the authority. But we might also add the neo-Calvinist tradition of sphere sovereignty, which, while flattening Arendt's pyramid, nonetheless manifests and preserves relationships of authority, not of force.

All of this is to emphasize, and put into clearer analytical and contemporary context, what Cicero and Augustine mean by duty and ordered relationships of command and obedience. When such relationships become oppressive (in the sense of coercive force—physical or psychological), they by definition cease to be authoritative. But when command and obedience are authoritative, they humanize, teach, and bind people together in relationships of mutual care. They achieve the harmony of a symphony of players rather than the unity of an onion.

In this, Hobbes's structure of authority is very much in the Ciceronian-Augustinian tradition. We constitute the sovereign power (either a single man or a body of men, as Hobbes says) voluntarily, in response to natural reason. Correspondingly, the sovereign authoritatively preserves the peace, using force only when the authority of the rational contract has broken down—when the lawbreaker ceases to honor his promise of obedience based on the authority of reason. What Hobbes sets in motion, however, is the inversion of right and law. More specifically, whereas Cicero and Augustine emphasize duty, the followers of Hobbes emphasize rights at the expense of duty. The followers of Hobbes view social life through the lens of rights, as a counterpoint to the breakdown of social life organized on principles of duty. Hobbes's overall framework defines the predicament that Cicero and Augustine saw, but from the other side: how to steer between too much authority on the one hand and too much liberty on the other. If the followers of Hobbes and the doctrine of rights sought to steer the ship of social life through the passage, they veered toward liberty, with the support of self-limitation yielding over time to license. Cicero and Augustine steered toward authority, tempered by the rational, emotional, and spiritual duties of care which, over time, were corrupted by the lust for domination.

But the contours of social life remain our own: what is the balance between private liberty and public constraint, on the one hand, and public liberty and private constraint on the other? How do we come to view social life not through the telescope of rights or authority, but through the binoculars of both, to render the complexity of social life in a three-dimensional perspective? Is it possible to recover a texture of social life based on non-oppressive hierarchical relationships of authority understood in terms of duties of care?

While Hobbes makes a great effort to show that his conception of social life is consistent with Christian doctrine, his project is nonetheless fundamentally secular. Ecclesiastical and temporal power are unified, for Hobbes, but on universal rational, material grounds.

If Hobbes makes a materialist turn, Jean Calvin—who also melds ecclesiastical and temporal power—orients his thinking in fundamentally spiritual terms. As with Hobbes, Calvin's method is fundamentally epistemological. The *Institutes* begins with epistemology, but unlike Aquinas's *Summa*, for example, never departs, leaving an ontology and theology of creation to one side. By contrast, Augustine takes ontology as his starting point, and derives his epistemology and moral philosophy accordingly.

For Calvin, as for Augustine, nature is a book to be read alongside scripture. But nature, and God's action in nature and history, seem for Calvin to be conceived primarily in terms of efficient causality. If Hobbes's system leans heavily on material and efficient causality, Calvin's rests primarily on efficient and final causality. Formal causality, whether in created nature or redemptive history, seems wholly absent in Calvin. God seems to act exclusively in terms of efficient causality. It is God's glory and majesty that have Calvin's attention, not God's beauty and the beauty of God's creation. Our becoming like God seems to be a function of our knowledge (the enlightenment of our often willful ignorance) rather than the healing of our souls to wholeness. Christ, says Calvin, is the material cause of our redemption.

What does it mean to situate a theology, and especially a theology of law and redemption primarily within a framework of material and efficient causality? To be sure, our final cause for Calvin is fellowship with God in divine peace, but in practice it would seem that we are not so much drawn upward to God as pushed by His glory and majesty as an efficient cause. Absent a strong account of formal causality, Calvin's doctrine cannot emphasize the natural and social whole.

Calvin quotes Augustine in the *Institutes* more than any other author. But even his use of Augustine is emblematic of Calvin's disposition toward epistemology and efficient causality. Quotations are used essentially as proof texts, and the whole structure of Augustine's thinking does not shine through. Calvin deploys select matter, but has neglected the form. Indeed, this neglect of form and emphasis on efficient and material cause lead Calvin to the problematic conclusion of double predestination, which Augustine avoids.

To reinforce his point that forgiveness of sins and justification are the same, Calvin invokes Augustine: "The righteousness of the saints in this world consists more in the forgiveness of sins than the perfection of virtue" (IN 3.22, p. 58, citing CG 19.27). As a matter of fact, Calvin has used Augustine well—our journey toward the perfection of virtue is partial at best. But Calvin has reversed the direction of Augustine's moral philosophy, which is, as we have seen, the pursuit of virtue aided by grace, not the covering of sin because virtue cannot be attained. Calvin quotes *City of God* Book 19 at least thirteen times in the *Institutes*, and yet the structure of Augustine's thinking, especially concerning the centrality of peace, seems invisible.

In the paragraph which follows the quotation from Augustine, Calvin cites Ambrose: "errors of conduct are covered by the brightness of faith," as an illustration of faith, not works, leading to justification—Jacob takes on the pleasant-smelling garments of his brother and so, in impersonating his brother, his own failings are covered up, a graceful deception which earns him a birthright he does not deserve. (IN 3.23, p. 59, quoting from Ambrose, *On Jacob and the Happy Life*, 2.2). Again, the passage is exemplary of Calvin's use of texts; and I note this not to criticize Calvin as a reader and writer, but as illustrative of his mode of thought—focused on epistemology and efficient causality, the focus on the part even as the *Institutes* constitutes an extraordinary achievement as a whole.

For Calvin, righteousness is directed toward justification. For Augustine, righteousness is directed toward virtue. For Calvin, our sins are cloaked in God's forgiveness, which is a function of God's majesty and magnanimity; for Augustine and Ambrose, our woundedness is healed by God the Physician, even if, on earth in time, that healing remains provisional. Augustine's reliance on formal causality allows him a conception of virtue that is not available to Calvin. What Augustine sees as the beauty of the whole becomes reduced in Calvin to the logic of the part—ontology and aesthetics are replaced by epistemology and logic, respectively. In Calvin, the part serves God's glory by being the object of efficient causality; in Augustine, the part is formed and re-formed to complete God's created beauty.

Again, the brushstrokes are broad; the aim is to illustrate the narrative lines of the poem we have inherited. The spirit of Hobbes and the spirit of Calvin, then, displace Augustine's conception of right and righteousness. Right and righteousness become unbound from an ontology of beauty and are confined to the fields of epistemology and logic. Reason as a formal cause is pushed aside in favor of will as an efficient cause. Indeed, paradoxically, the modern spirit subordinates reason to will.

In Hobbes, reason puts itself in service of human will—before the institution of the sovereign to keep everyone in awe there is no justice. For Calvin, God's justification is not a function of God's reason or of the order of creation, but of God's will. Law and grace, then, become functions of will—in this sense both are arbitrary. For Hobbes and Calvin, law is an expression of reason subordinated to will derived from epistemology. For Augustine, law is an expression of will subordinated to reason formed by ontology. Unbound from created nature, law loses its connection to beauty.

As a result, in both its material and spiritual forms, modern positive law suffers from a contradiction. On the one hand, the principle of law is held to be a rational command which applies equally to all. On the other hand, detached from an anchor—perhaps in nature, perhaps in God—that principle is relative, an expression simply of will, of power. So long as the law does not contradict itself—is not logically incoherent in substance or process—at any given time, it is understood to be valid. As an expression of will, the law is changeable with respect to will—either the will of one or of many—and so is unbounded by circumstance.

Though distinct from Kant, this vision of positive law nonetheless privileges only part of Kant's philosophy. Specifically, it embraces the *Critique of Pure Reason*, while neglecting the *Critique of Judgment*. Kant's categorical imperative, articulated in the *Critique of Pure Reason*, asks us always to act in such a manner that the principle of our action can become a universal law. Such an imperative subordinates individual circumstances which are necessarily unique, to a general, rational law. Thus, the categorical imperative, grounded in reason, asks me to consider the consistency and uniformity of creation—its sameness and not its difference—as the reference point for judging my actions and the world.

In the *Critique of Judgment*, however, Kant pursues a different argument. Here, rational agreement with oneself is replaced with the ability "to think in the place of everybody else"; that is, to see the world from the point of view of other creatures. To do so, Kant says, is to create "an enlarged mentality." The activity of judgment, unlike that of pure reason, forces me out of the "subjective private conditions" which characterize my opinions and desires. It reminds me that I do not exist in social or natural isolation, but as a free agent who is not autonomous—not a law unto myself, a free agent who is properly free to act in such a way that both myself and others become more ourselves—as individual, not generic, representatives of the species. (CC pp. 219–21).

Augustine asks us to consider each decision in the knowledge of our place in all of creation, and with a love proper to all creatures—to see and love the world, and our place in it as a whole ... as God sees it, as best we can with our limited perception and shabby moral equipment. We are created to learn, not only in the knowledge of ourselves and other creatures, but with the love that comes from seeing each as they are—in their number, measure, and weight, and in what fruit they might bear for the whole. The music of the word places our ethical framework in an aesthetic framework—in placing my feet in the poem of creation I have to consider not only my own number, measure, and weight, but also the number, measure, and weight of those around me, in relation to those who have come before and those who shall come afterward. I do so with faith and hope, composing my contributions to the verse within my necessarily limited comprehension of the verse as a whole. We are cultivating seeds which we inherited, and nurturing trees under whose shade we may never sit.

The verse is a halting one, like a mosaic full of smooth and jagged edged pieces, syllables that trip the tongue, feet that step on the toes of others, jostling the soul—and yet the grace of Christ, the tuner of tuners, the measurer of feet, sustains the music of the word to moments of purity amid the cacophony of time. Non-human creatures live and die with the periodic regularities of time, the basso continuo of creation over which human beings—uniquely graced with moral freedom—play their discordant melodies. And yet, creation bends those melodies to itself, to the harmony that even the most sinful souls find hard to resist—the lesser beauties are beauties nonetheless, and like Christ tune the strings of human time to a common key.

The capacity to judge, not simply to reason, is a specifically political ability, says Hannah Arendt, namely the ability to see things not only from one's own point of view but in the perspective of all those who happen to be present; even that judgment may be one of the fundamental abilities of humans as political beings insofar as it enables us to orient ourselves in the public realm

(CC p. 221). Arendt goes on to remark that it was when Kant was examining the phenomenon of taste—understood as an attentive relationship to the beautiful—that he discovered that judging is perhaps the most important activity "in which this sharing-the-world-with-others comes to pass." Taste is usually understood to rest beyond the realm of politics and the sphere of reason, as are aesthetic matters in general. Nonetheless, Arendt argues,

> In aesthetic no less than in political judgments, a decision is made, and although this decision is always determined by a certain subjectivity, by the simple fact that each person occupies a place of his own from which he looks upon and judges the world, it also derives from the fact that the world itself is an objective datum, something common to all its inhabitants. The activity of taste decides how this world, independent of its utility and our vital interests in it, is to look and sound, what men will see and what they will hear in it. Taste judges the world in its appearance and in its worldliness; its interest in the world is purely "disinterested," and that means that neither the life interests of the individual nor the moral interests of the self are involved here. For judgments of taste, the world is the primary thing, not man, neither man's life nor his self. (CC p. 222).

Augustine would embrace the aesthetic character of political judgment, indeed of all judgment, but would revise this last sentence, for in his view of creation "primary" belongs to number or rhythm. The world may be the verse wherein our life and self disclose themselves in metrical feet, but it is precisely within that verse that we come to the fullness of our individual meaning. Numerical primacy gives way to the proportional equality of meter.

We are, of course, voices speaking the syllables of meter simultaneously; not only our individual lines but our collective narrative are unrehearsed and un-conducted, save insofar as we respond to the common intimations of the natural laws of creation. Politics, then, becomes the collective persuasive negotiation of syllables in time and space. Politics do not primarily concern knowledge or truth, as though theoretical proofs tell us what to do. Politics concerns judgment, decision, and action.

Culture and politics, then, belong together because it is not knowledge or truth which is at stake, but rather judgment and decision, the judicious exchange of opinion about the sphere of public life and the common world, and the decision what manner of action is to be taken in it, as well as to how it is to look henceforth, what kind of things are to appear in it. (CC p. 223)

It is for this reason Arendt (elsewhere, in her essay "What Is Freedom?") will describe certain political moments as miraculous, as creation ex nihilo. Augustine would not go quite so far, insisting that God alone has the capacity to create from nothing. But Augustine and Arendt agree that there are marvels of human creativity in which old materials are formed anew in unprecedented ways.

Reason, then, is put in service of miracles, miracles which interrupt the poem without being discontinuous with it. For miracles are also the refinements of our perceptions. Just as Kant's Critiques move from pure reason, to practical reason, to judgment, Augustine's analysis places number-rhythm, measure, and meter within verse, the weight of love. It is the realm of aesthetic judgment where freedom comes to rest, where we weigh our competing, restless loves, where not only the mind but also the heart is enlarged in the ever-active relationship with beauty. The law of liberty is the law of love when the judgments of taste proceed from the reasons of the heart.

Postlude

The many wonders of human creativity in history are no less awe-inspiring and terrifying than the miracles of nature. The actions of human beings are in fact the actions of creation upon itself. Yet no creature seems to have greater powers of freedom in action, pulled as we are both upward and outward—and downward and inward. The blessing and curse of being human is always to be freely in between, and so never free of responsibility. Our impatience in failing to wait for the light leads us into the darkness of pride, and what is properly creative turns the power of making into acts of destruction. Are we really torn between the freedom to submit and the freedom to subjugate? The dog and the horse obey our commands; the cat does not. But the dog and horse obey freely, and they forgive. There are no bad dogs or horses, only bad owners. When we diminish them, we diminish ourselves. When we uplift them, they uplift our souls—both species reach heights together which they could never reach singly. So too with our fellow human beings. When bound together by law and love, we have the possibility of becoming our greater selves; self-sufficiency in spirit as well as in matter requires that we depend upon one another, upon nature, upon God. To depend: literally, to hang down—to be suspended by, to wait, or be in suspense. To rely upon another is to live in strength, not weakness; to depend is to be uplifted, not dragged down. To be bound together in law and love is to be bound by the radiant fibers of care.

And yet the ties that bind us often do not lift us up; bound inwardly to ourselves we sink, losing our place, crushing those we suppose to be beneath us. Out of law we are willing to kill; in love we are willing to die. What are the patterns of timeless moments that shape the power of love over the love of power? Patterns form but do not determine the shape of history; to live and learn in patterns is to participate as a part in a whole, not as cogs in a machine but as fronds unfurling on the fern.

If, as the poet tells us, history is a pattern of timeless moments, then nature is the pattern of moments in time. A people is redeemed only in the attunement of the poem of history to the poem of nature, spelling out the chord that spells creation. Without beauty we are all poor, and a faith without beauty is doubly impoverished. Faith is not what we believe, or what we believe in, but that by which we believe, sings Augustine. Faith is the "how" of beauty, lost in the shaft of sunlight, or the sage upon the western hillside in the warmth that follows an afternoon rain. Love has a song. Only the lover sings. Do we play the arts of living mechanistically, or virtuosically, by ear? Are the strings of our souls well tuned?

As we move forward in a wood, we see new trees and leave others behind, but the forest itself is never wholly seen—it recedes just beyond where we are, and so we are never precisely certain of our location. Ortega y Gasset introduces this image in his note to the reader of his *Meditations on Quixote*, illustrating the predicament of our limited perspective. "When shall we open our minds," he continues,

> to the conviction that the ultimate reality of the world is neither matter nor spirit, is no definite thing, but a perspective? God is perspective and hierarchy; Satan's sin was an error of perspective. Now, a perspective is perfected by the multiplication of its viewpoints and the precision with which we react to each one of its planes. The intuition of higher values fertilizes our contact with the lesser ones, and love for what is near and small makes the sublime real and effective within our hearts. For the person for whom small things do not exist, the great is not great. (MQ pp. 44, 45)

Both Plato and Ortega speak of learning as a species of hunting, in that the pursuer aims at the capture. But every noble capture is preceded by a change in perspective—one learns to see the quarry from the quarry's point of view. In riding a horse or training a dog, one unlearns one's own perspective in order to be united with the other in a mutual perspective which enlarges the individual personality of each without annihilating either. Learning and loving another is a dance of openness and conviction, not a possession but an expansion of love beyond desire. One may lead, another may follow, and the pattern may change with time and circumstance, now leading, now following, united in a faith in one another and the whole, a faith that passes all understanding, like a chorus which sings the chords of creation. And you are the music while the music lasts.

We cannot put sight in blind eyes, says Plato. But there must be an art by which we can shift another's gaze, help refocus their perspective (and our own). This is nothing less than the turning of the whole soul in which the soul learns to see again, to hear again, the music that has been there all along. Our experimental wanderings with Augustine have been essays—a sallying forth—in perspective, a Quixotic hope in the vitality of the soul. An adventure in loving is not a presentation of answers, but rather an opportunity to become more pure in our loves. For the object of love presents itself more fully only to the lover who is receptive, and receptivity depends upon an enlarged capacity for perspective. A narrowed perspective seeks answers; our answers are only as good as our questions, and we only attend to objects appropriate to the instrument by which we observe and measure them. We do not use a thermometer to measure velocity, or a ruler to measure temperature. By what instrument do we measure the arts of living well? The desiccation of the world of thought, the constriction of vitality that anesthetizes our age has much to do with the limitation of the tools by which we view and measure the world, the narrowing of our field of vision.

By placing the good and the true under the canopy of the beautiful, Augustine expands our field of vision and demands that we measure the world and ourselves with the fullness of our souls. He asks us to abandon our enchantments with power and be restored to the ecology of justice. What begins with the binding of the law culminates in the ligaments of love. For love binds us to things not in the safeguarding of rights but in the honoring of responsibilities.

You who are beyond all naming, who gives form to all things, aligns the axes of the world, wraps the day with the comforting vestments of dawn's beauteous light, and envelopes the night with the gracious comforts of slumber, You do so that our aching joints might be restored for useful service, and that our wearied minds may be uplifted—our whole being released from anxiety and grief, ushered to the tranquility of the Sabbath rest. Gratitude is a form of knowledge, and wisdom finds its culmination in gratitude to You.

Perhaps our time with Augustine has restored some of the inner warmth to our reading and writing, expanding our "radius of sympathy" for the small and the great of creation and of history. If, in our state of exile, we have a greater desire for pilgrimage, our journey with Augustine will have been worth the time. If the interwoven song of nature and of history is more harmonious, the reasons of the heart have more room to present themselves in the simplicity of their gift. The pilgrim recognizes—sees and thinks again—the created simplicity of what has been present all along. The refinement of our perceptions allows us to receive rather than possess, to embrace rather than dominate. If we do not see the things of creation in the fullness of their measure, number, and weight, it is because they do not find in us the multifaceted surface in which to be reflected. Our journey with Augustine is not the hero's journey home, but the pilgrim's quest to polish the surface of the soul. In perfecting our capacity for love, we perfect our capacity to love others in the fullest unfoldment of their creative potential. This is the expansion of love beyond desire, for desire seeks to possess, while love rests in delight. The poem of the universe resolves itself in that great, inexpressible cacophony of joy.

BIBLIOGRAPHY

Against the Academicians and The Teacher. King, Peter, trans. Indianapolis, IN: Hackett, 1995.
Arendt, Hannah. "What Is Authority?" and "The Crisis in Culture" in *Between Past and Future: Eight Exercises in Political Thought*. New York: Viking Press, 1968.
Aristotle. *Nicomachean Ethics*. Bartlett, Robert C. and Collins, Susan D., trans. Chicago: University of Chicago Press, 2012.
Calvin, John. *The Institutes of the Christian Religion*. Beveridge, Henry, trans. Grand Rapids, MI: Wm. B. Eerdmans Publishing Co., 1989.
Cicero. *On Duties*. Griffin, M. T. and Atkins, E. M., eds. and trans. Cambridge: Cambridge University Press, 1991.
The City of God Against the Pagans. Dyson, R. W., trans. Cambridge: Cambridge University Press, 1998.
The Confessions of St. Augustine. Warner, Rex, trans. New York: Signet, 1963.
Constant, Benjamin. *Political Writings*. Fontana, Biancamaria, trans. Cambridge: Cambridge University Press, 1988.
Hobbes, Thomas. *Man and Citizen (De Homine and De Cive)*. Gert, Bernard, ed. Wood, Charles T. and Scott-Craig, T. S. K., trans. Indianapolis, IN: Hackett, 1991.
The Literal Meaning of Genesis/St. Augustine. 2 vols. Taylor, John Hammond, trans. and ed. Ancient Christian Writers Series, vols. 41–42. New York: Newman Press, 1982.
On Free Choice of Will. Benjamin, A. S. and Hackstaff, L. H., trans. Indianapolis, IN: Bobbs-Merrill, 1964.
On Music. Schopp, Ludwig, trans. in The Fathers of the Church, vol. 4, 1947.
The Trinity. Hill, Edmund, trans. New York: New City Press, 1998.

FURTHER READING

Books, like friends, do not present themselves in an orderly fashion. Our minds and souls are fed by what we read, and like food, the nourishment is of varying quality. We metabolize, synthesize, accept, reject, and modify what we read and at a certain point the result is that common dish: the stew, or goulash, or feijoada … the mixture which, like a poem or a piece of music, takes what is at hand and makes something delicious of it. Similarly, when we undertake a journey, we are left with a host of impressions, experiences, sensations that cease to have a chronological order. Many of the works which follow have been lifelong companions; others have been more immediately present to the writing of this book. Some are included here because of their content; others because of their content and their assistance in reflection on the form of writing and thinking. The suggestions presented here are not intended in lieu of footnotes; they are intended as further companions for explorations into charted territory, and landscapes as yet unknown.

Prelude

Fermor, Patrick Leigh. *A Time to Keep Silence*. New York: New York Review Books, 2007.
Hadot, Pierre. *Philosophy as a Way of Life: Spiritual Exercises from Socrates to Foucault*. Arnold Davidson, ed. Michael Chase, trans. Oxford: Blackwell, 1995.
Kierkegaard, Søren. *Purity of Heart Is to Will One Thing*. Steere, Douglas V., trans. New York: HarperOne, 1956.
Mann, Thomas. *Doctor Faustus: The Life of the German Composer Adrian Leverkühn*. Woods, John E. trans. New York: Knopf Doubleday, 1999.
Maclean, Norman. *A River Runs Through It and Other Stories*. Chicago: University of Chicago Press, 1976.
Marion, Jean-Luc. *God Without Being: Hors-Texte*. Carlson, Thomas A., trans. Chicago: University of Chicago Press, 1995.

Pieper, Josef. *Only the Lover Sings: Art and Contemplation*. Krauth, Lothar, trans. San Francisco: Ignatius Press, 1990.
Pieper, Josef. *Leisure, the Basis of Culture*. Dru, Alexander, trans. Indianapolis, IN: Liberty Fund, 1999.
Śarma, Visnu. *The Pañcatantra*. Rajan, Chandra, trans. New York: Penguin Books, 1993.

Chapter 1: Echoes of Creation

Burnell, Peter. *The Augustinian Person*. Washington, DC: Catholic University of America Press, 2005.
Darwin, Charles. *The Descent of Man*. New York: Penguin, 2004.
Hearne, Vicki. *Adam's Task: Calling Animals by Name*. New York: Alfred A. Knopf, 1986.
Heschel, Abraham Joshua. *The Sabbath*. New York: Farrar, Straus and Giroux, 1996.
Kass, Leon R. *Toward a More Natural Science: Biology and Human Affairs*. New York: Free Press, 1985.

Chapter 2: The Actor in History

Berry, Wendell. *Standing by Words: Essays*. Berkeley: Counterpoint, 1983.
Eliot, T. S. *Four Quartets*. New York: Harcourt Brace Jovanovich, 1943.
Summers, David. *The Judgment of Sense: Renaissance Naturalism and the Rise of Aesthetics*. Cambridge: Cambridge University Press, 1987.
Summers, David. *Michelangelo and the Language of Art*. Princeton: Princeton University Press, 1981.

Chapter 3: Righteousness Unbound

Gomá Lanzón, Javier. Ejemplaridad pública (Tetralogía de la Ejemplaridad). Madrid: Taurus, 2010.
Manent, Pierre. *City of Man*. LePain, Marc A., trans. Princeton: Princeton University Press, 1998.
Niebuhr, Reinhold. *The Nature and Destiny of Man, Vol. 1, Human Nature*. New York: Charles Scribner's Sons, 1941/1964.
Taylor, Joshua C. *Learning to Look: A Handbook for the Visual Arts*. Chicago: University of Chicago Press, 1981.

Chapter 4: Imagined Communities

Meier, Heinrich. *Leo Strauss and the Theological-Political Problem.* Brainard, Marcus, trans. Cambridge: Cambridge University Press, 2006.
O'Donovan, O. M. T. *Common Objects of Love: Moral Reflection and the Shaping of Community.* Grand Rapids, MI: William B. Eerdmans Publishing, 2002.
Taylor, Charles. *Modern Social Imaginaries.* Durham: Duke University Press, 2004.
Weil, Simone. *The Need for Roots: Prelude to a Declaration of Duties Toward Mankind.* Wills, Arthur, trans. (with a preface by T. S. Eliot). New York: G. P. Putnam's Sons, 1952.

Chapter 5: The Arc of Justice and the Arrow of Beauty

Hearne, Vicki. *Tricks of the Light: New and Selected Poems.* Hollander, John, ed. Chicago: University of Chicago Press, 2007.
Hopkins, Gerard Manley. *Gerard Manley Hopkins: The Major Works.* Catherine Phillips, ed. New York: Oxford University Press, 2002.
McMahon, Robert. *Augustine's Prayerful Ascent: An Essay on the Literary Form of the Confessions.* Athens: University of Georgia Press, 1989.
Ratzinger, Joseph Cardinal. *On the Way to Jesus Christ.* Miller, Michael J., trans. San Francisco: Ignatius Press, 2005.
von Balthasar, Hans Urs. *Love Alone Is Credible.* Schindler, D. C., trans. San Francisco: Ignatius Press, 2004.

Chapter 6: The Music of the Word

Mill, John Stuart. *On Liberty.* New York: Macmillan, 1956.
Murray, Albert. *The Hero and the Blues.* New York: Vintage Books, 1995.
Plato, *The Laws of Plato.* Pangle, Thomas L., trans. New York: Basic Books, Inc., 1980.
Plotinus, *Enneads.* McKenna, Stephen, trans. Burdett, NY: Larson Publications, 1992.

Chapter 7: The Law of Liberty and the Law of Love

Asad, Muhammad. *This Law of Ours, and Other Essays*. Kuala Lumpur: Islamic Book Trust, 2001.
Camus, Albert. *The Plague*. New York: Vintage International, 1991.
Cather, Willa. *Death Comes for the Archbishop*. New York: Vintage Classics, 1990.
Habermas, Jürgen. *An Awareness of What Is Missing: Faith and Reason in a Post-Secular Age*. Cronin, Ciaran, trans. Malden, MA: Polity Press, 2010.
Oakeshott, Michael. *On Human Conduct*. Oxford: Clarendon Press, 1975.
Shakespeare, William. *Measure for Measure*. New York: Simon and Schuster, 2005.
Simon, Yves. *Nature and Functions of Authority*. Aquinas Lecture for 1940. Milwaukee, WI: Marquette University Press, 1948.
Tierney, Brian. *The Idea of Natural Rights: Studies on Natural Rights, Natural Law, and Church Law, 1150–1625*. Atlanta: Scholars Press, 1997.
Tuck, Richard. *Natural Rights Theories: Their Origin and Development*. Cambridge: Cambridge University Press, 1979.
Voegelin, Eric. *The New Science of Politics: An Introduction*. Chicago: University of Chicago Press, 1952.
Wojtyla, Karol. *Love and Responsibility*. Willetts, H. T., trans. New York: Farrar, Strauss, Giroux, 1981.

Postlude

Kierkegaard, Søren. *The Present Age*. Dru, Alexander, trans. New York: Harper and Row, 1962.
Ortega y Gasset, José. *Meditations on Quixote*. Rugg, Evelyn and Marín, Diego, trans. New York: W. W. Norton and Co., 1963.

www.ingramcontent.com/pod-product-compliance
Lightning Source LLC
Chambersburg PA
CBHW060955230426
43665CB00015B/2217